THE MARS CHALLENGE

ALISON WILGUS AND WYETH YATES

Dedicated to the hardworking engineers and scientists and space-policy advocates who have gotten us this far

First Second

Text copyright © 2020 Alison Wilgus
Illustrations copyright © 2020 Wyeth Yates

Published by First Second
First Second is an imprint of Roaring Brook Press, a division of Holtzbrinck Publishing Holdings Limited Partnership
120 Broadway, New York, NY 10271

Don't miss your next favorite book from First Second! For the latest updates go to firstsecondnewsletter.com and sign up for our enewsletter.

Library of Congress Control Number: 2019903649
Paperback ISBN: 978-1-62672-083-1
Hardcover ISBN: 978-1-250-25825-0

Our books may be purchased in bulk for promotional, educational, or business use. Please contact your local bookseller or the Macmillan Corporate and Premium Sales Department at (800) 221-7945 ext. 5442 or by email at MacmillanSpecialMarkets@macmillan.com.

First edition, 2020

Edited by Calista Brill, Robyn Chapman, and Hazel Newlevant
Cover design by Andrew Arnold and Kirk Benshoff
Lettering and interior book design by Chris Dickey
Expert consultation by Liz Warren, PhD, and Emily Lakdawalla
Printed in China by 1010 Printing International Limited, North Point, Hong Kong

Penciled with a blue Prismacolor Col-Erase pencil. Inked with a Winsor & Newton Series 7 brush, Tachikawa Maru nibs, and Faber-Castell Pitt pens. Colored in Photoshop.

Paperback: 10 9 8 7 6 5 4 3 2 1
Hardcover: 10 9 8 7 6 5 4 3 2 1

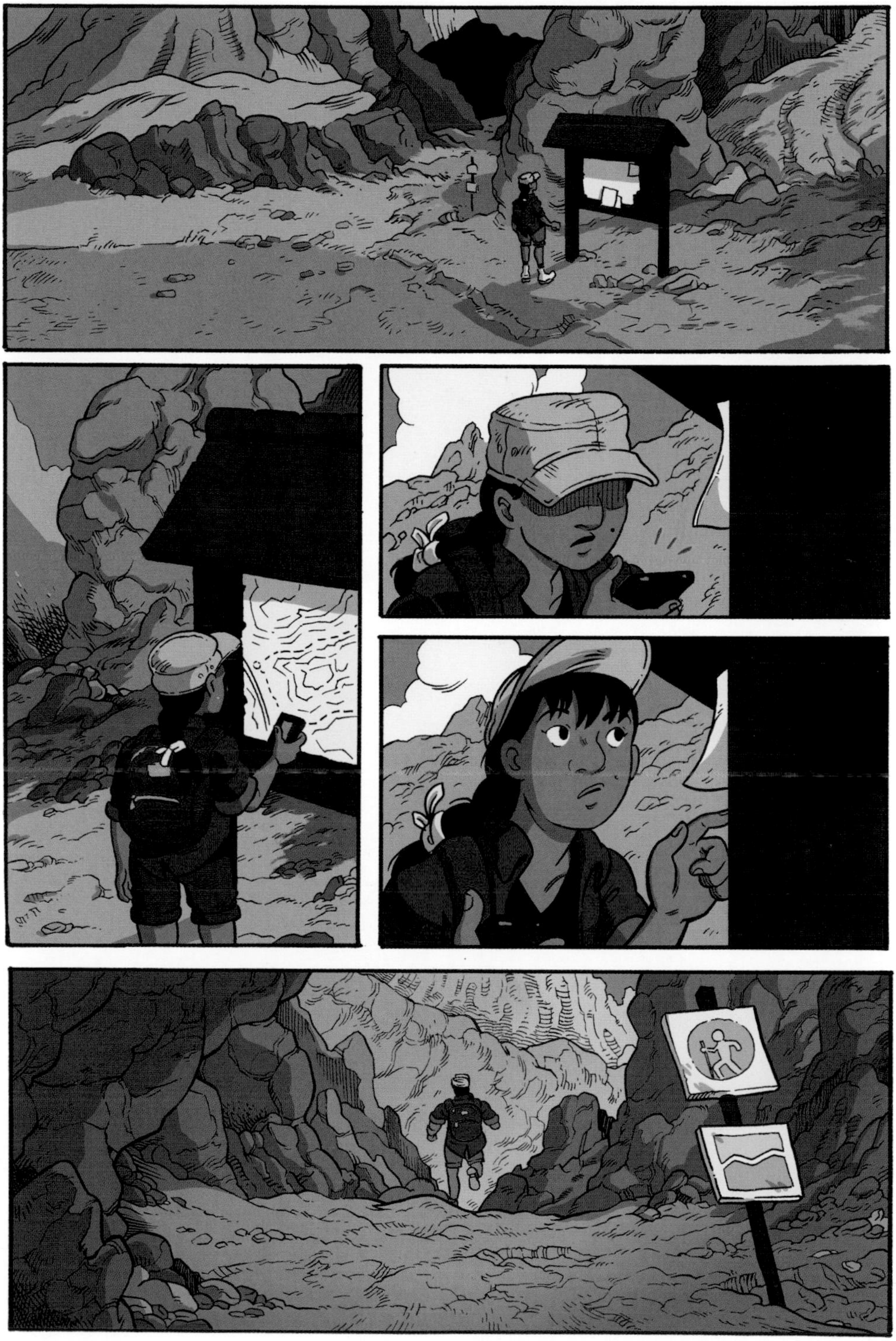

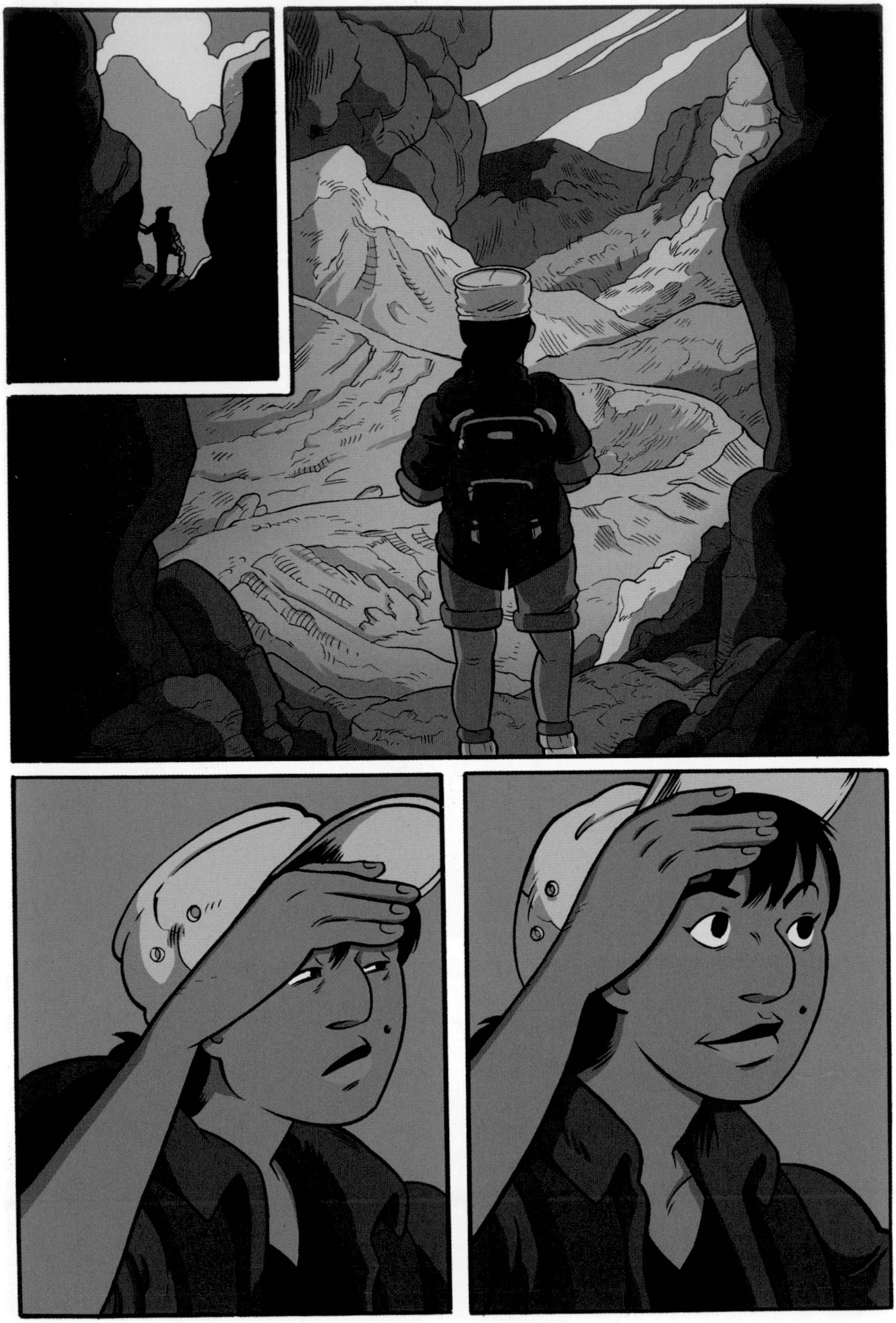

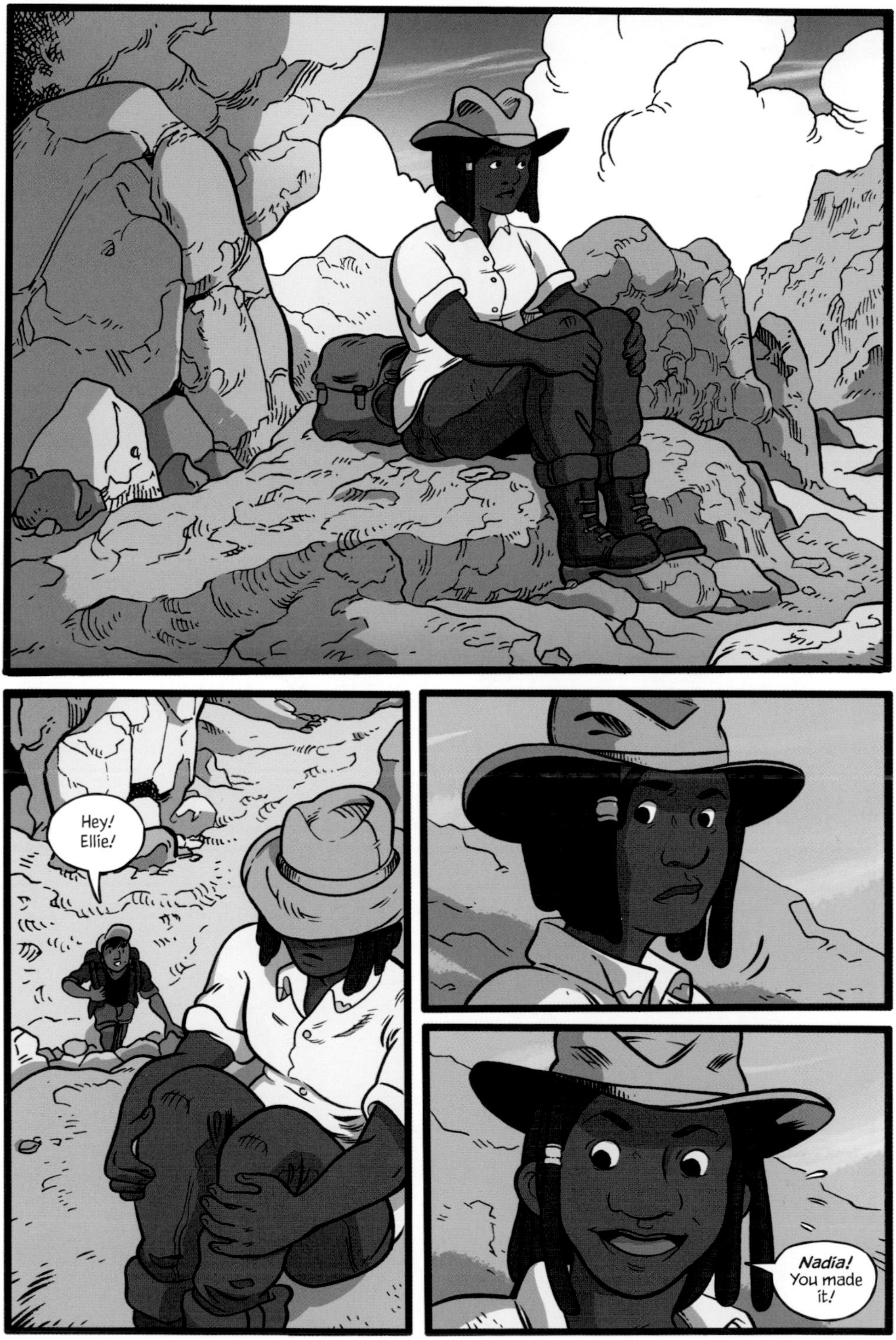
Hey! Ellie!
Nadia! You made it!

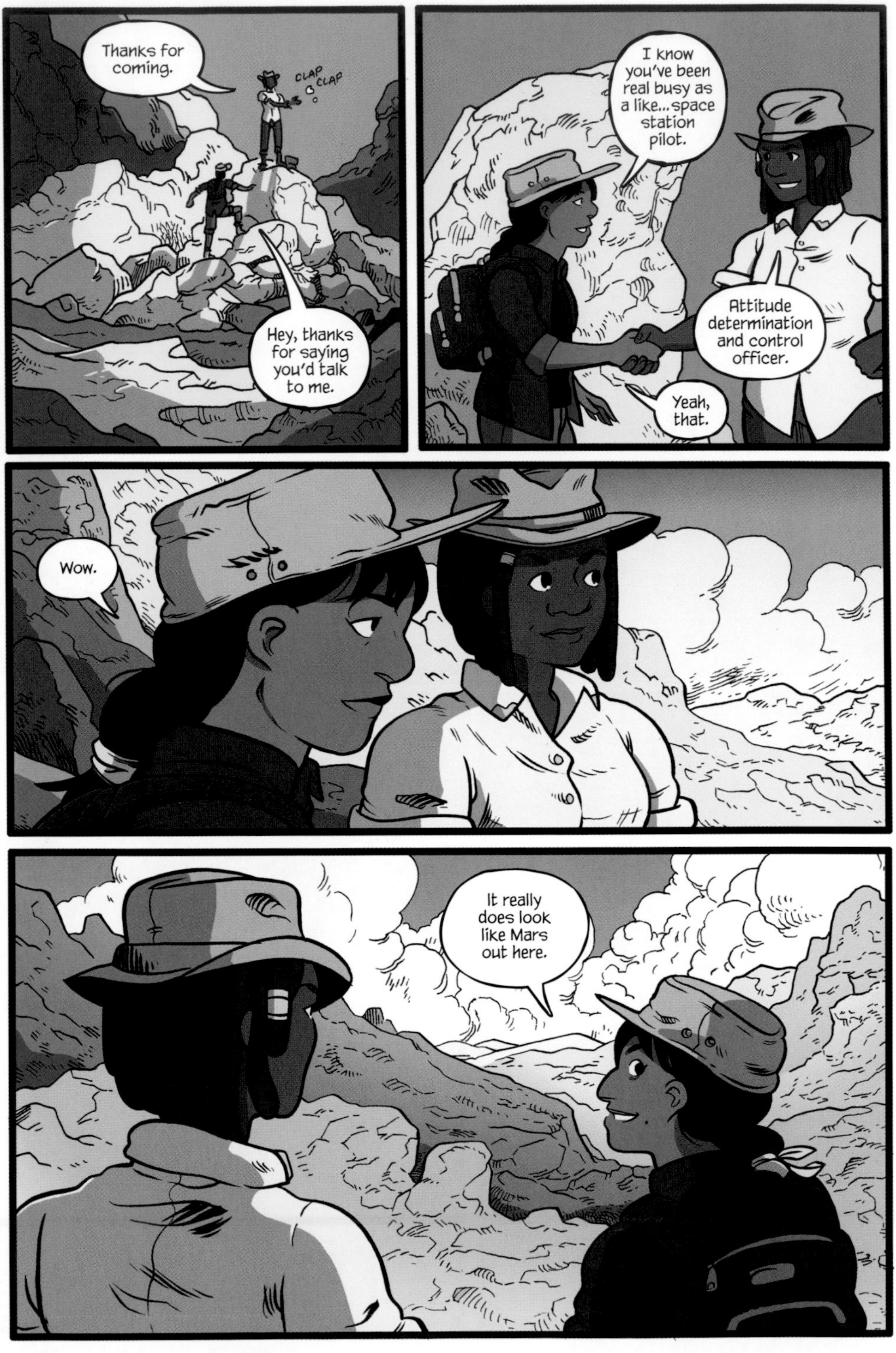
Thanks for coming.
CLAP CLAP
Hey, thanks for saying you'd talk to me.
I know you've been real busy as a like... space station pilot.
Attitude determination and control officer.
Yeah, that.
Wow.
It really does look like Mars out here.

So, hey! Human spaceflight!

Heck yeah.

Still aiming to join the first mission to Mars?

Double heck yeah.

So this is early reconnaissance for you.

If I'm gonna be the first woman on Mars, I figure I should know my stuff, right?

They'll want a well-rounded candidate.

Well, I am *honored* to be at your service.

I'm just a desk jockey myself, but I've picked up a few things.

So where do we start? Low-gravity maneuvers? Rocket science? Decompression first aid?

We start with a question.

Why the heck are we even trying to do this?

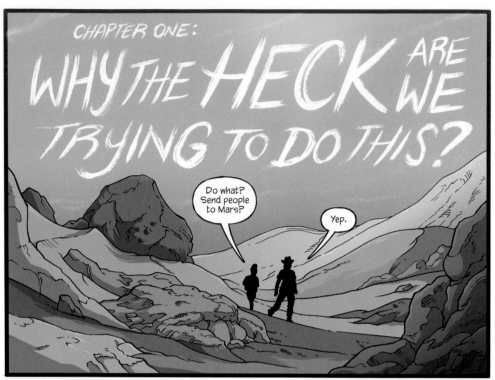

CHAPTER ONE:

WHY THE HECK ARE WE TRYING TO DO THIS?

Do what? Send people to Mars?

Yep.

Uhhhhh, because we obviously want to?

Who do you mean by *"we"*?

Everyone. Like, as a species, we are *super* into the idea of sending humans to Mars.

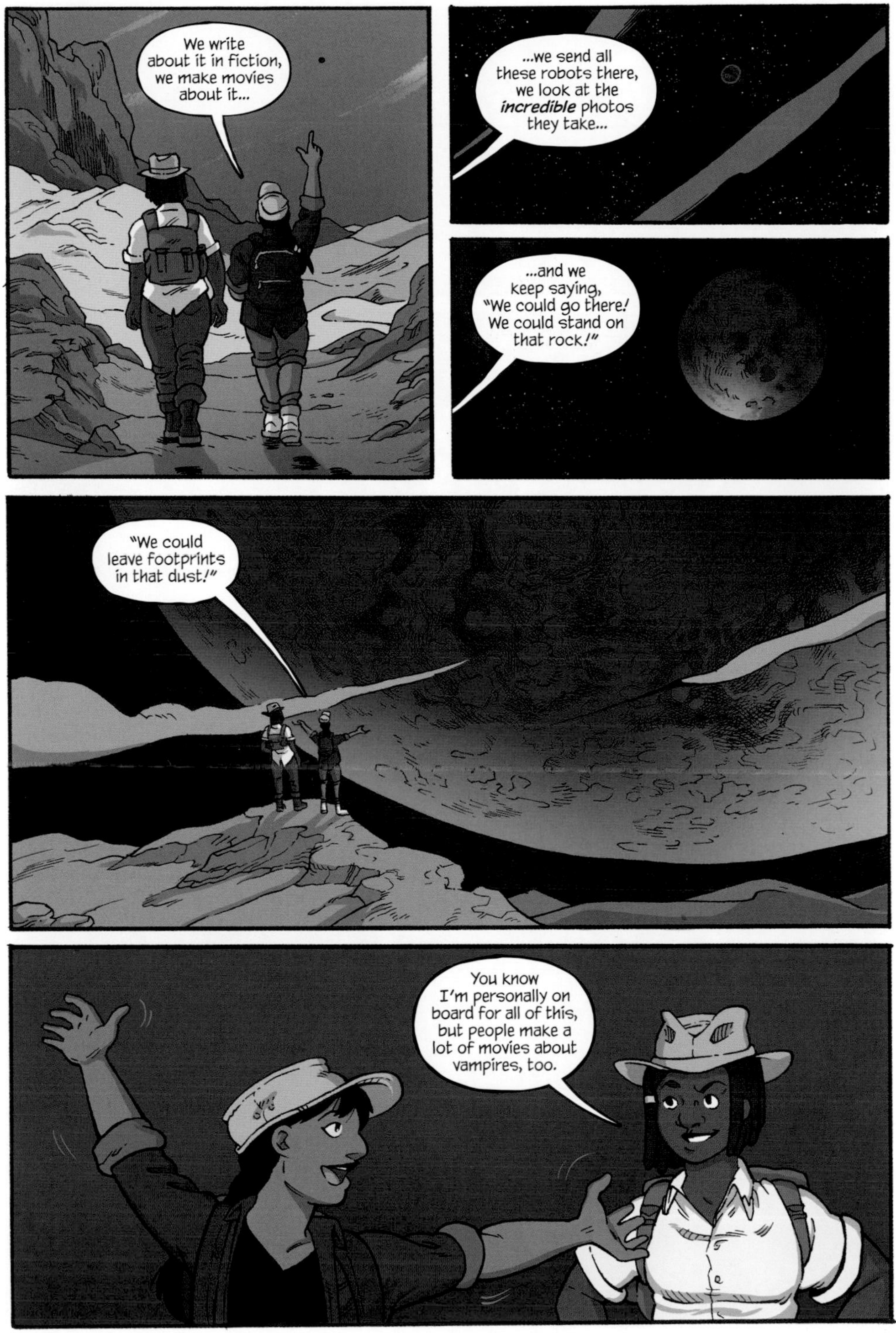
We write about it in fiction, we make movies about it...
...we send all these robots there, we look at the *incredible* photos they take...
...and we keep saying, "We could go there! We could stand on that rock!"
"We could leave footprints in that dust!"
You know I'm personally on board for all of this, but people make a lot of movies about vampires, too.

For *me*, when I read about going to Mars I'm thinking, "We have to do this! We have to make it happen!"

But I'll admit, I don't assume the average tax-payer thinks about it that way.

Other people *do* share in your human emotions, Eleanor.

Sure, but...

...if we want to get as many people on board as we can, shouldn't we be talking about the actual for-real important reasons for going to Mars?

You thinking of anything in particular?

Well, to start, we barely understand how anything works on Earth.

We only kind of know why we're this happy blue-and-green ball with a huge ecosystem, while Mars looks like a dead red rock with hardly any atmosphere, hardly any liquid water, hardly any *anything* you'd need to stay alive.

We know that there's water ice on Mars, and sometimes liquid brine when conditions are just right. We know the chemical makeup of some of the rocks and dust on the surface.

We know that solar wind—like the literal stream of charged particles that comes shooting out from the Sun—has been stripping Mars' air away for billions of years. And we know what the air that's left is made out of.

Now, most of this isn't stuff you can learn just by looking through a telescope on Earth.

We build robots to send to Mars and poke around for us. And each of those robots is designed to look for and measure very specific things.

Once a robot's launched... that's it!

Whadya mean, "That's it?" Some of those robots last a long time.

I mean look at *Opportunity*— it trucked around Mars for nearly fifteen years.

The Mars *Odyssey's* been in orbit and transmitting for more than fifteen!

Yes, but that means they're also stuck with old capabilities.

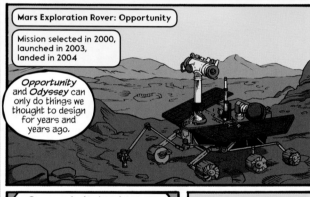

Mars Exploration Rover: Opportunity

Mission selected in 2000, launched in 2003, landed in 2004

Opportunity and *Odyssey* can only do things we thought to design for years and years ago.

So as our technology improves, and as we learn more about what Mars is really like and what questions we want to answer about it, those old robot explorers are kind of...

outdated.

That's some harsh rover shade you're throwing.

Oppy was a trouper and I would never speak ill of it.

Equipped with cameras, spectrometers, a rock abrasion tool, and an atmospheric dust analyzer.

But it was only designed to take photographs and to look at the very top layer of the Martian surface.

Even though, if there's any possibility of life on Mars...

...that life is almost definitely farther down in the regolith.

Down where there's ice and brine, and where there's some protection from radiation.

Pause. "Regolith"?

All-purpose word for "sand and dust and bits of rock."

And we wanna go digging into that stuff.

Yes! But we couldn't really manage that at all until we sent the Mars Science Lab—

Curiosity?

Yes! *Curiosity.* Which launched *eight years* after the Mars Exploration Rovers *Spirit* and *Opportunity.* Not exactly a quick turnaround.

Mars Science Laboratory: Curiosity

Mission selected in 2004, launched in 2011, landed in 2012

Hmm.

And even then, it is *super* limited in what it can do. Like, it can drill into rocks and scoop up a little bit of regolith to put into its instruments.

Equipped with cameras, spectrometers, a chromograph, a laser that vaporizes surface material for analysis, a radiation detector, and instruments for atmospheric monitoring.

But again, there could be Martian bacteria living six inches under the surface and we'd have a really, *really* hard time finding it with the robots sitting on Mars right now.

Our best bet would be to luck into the rover being very close to a fresh impact crater, and even then—

Whatever we found would've just been hit by a meteor.

Yep.

I think I'm starting to see where you're going with this.

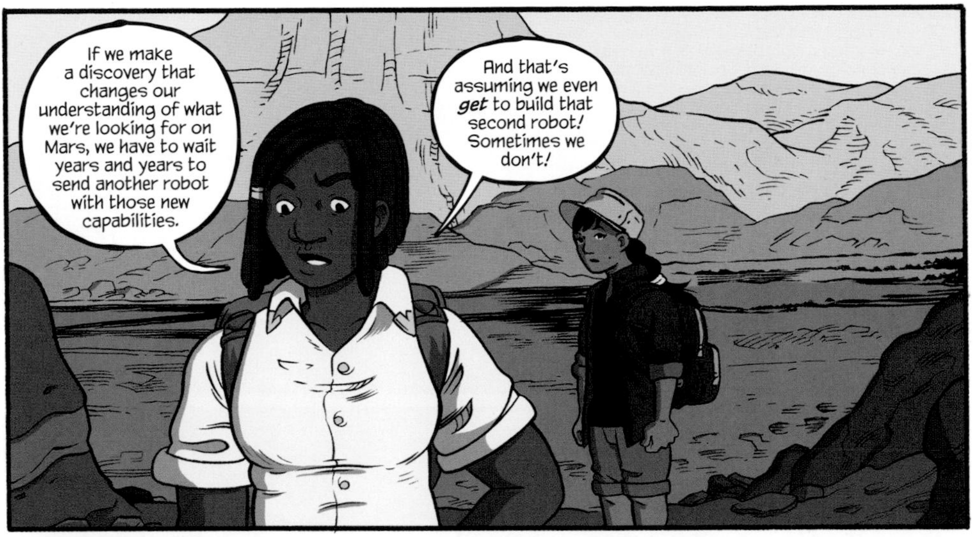
If we make a discovery that changes our understanding of what we're looking for on Mars, we have to wait years and years to send another robot with those new capabilities.
And that's assuming we even ***get*** to build that second robot! Sometimes we don't!

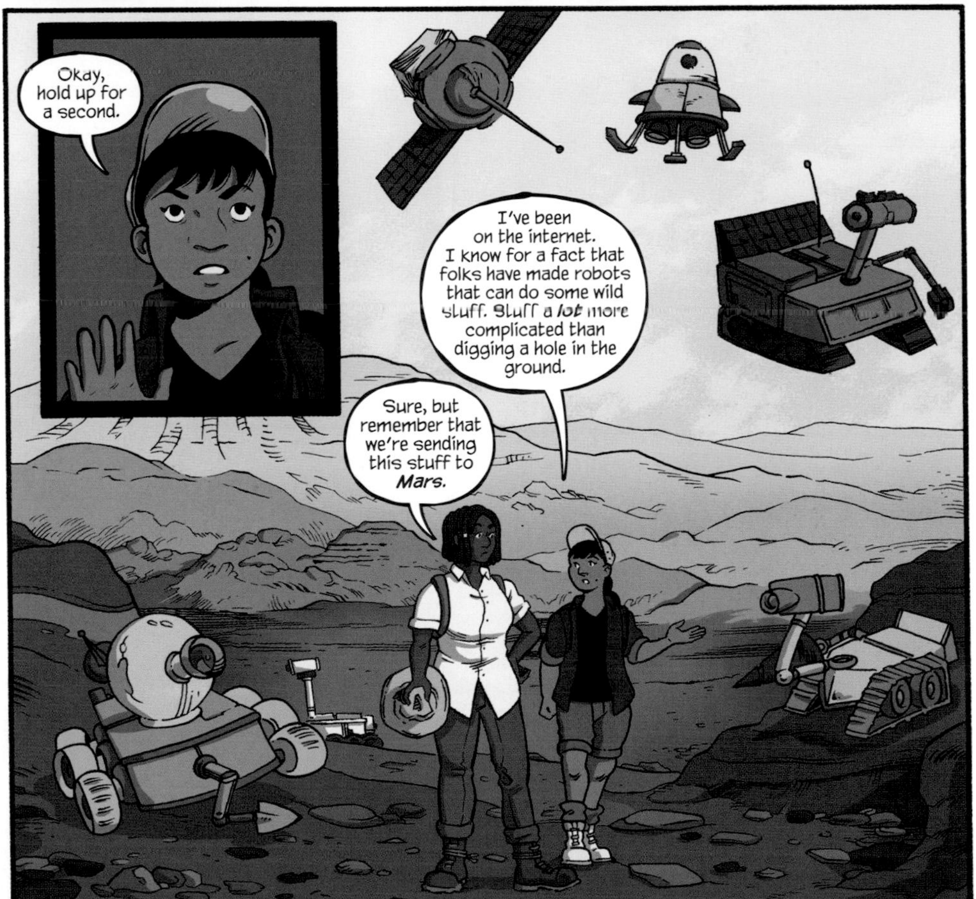
Okay, hold up for a second.
I've been on the internet. I know for a fact that folks have made robots that can do some wild stuff. Stuff a ***lot*** more complicated than digging a hole in the ground.
Sure, but remember that we're sending this stuff to ***Mars.***

We could send the fanciest possible hole-digging robot, but what if it fell over and couldn't get back up again? What if its little robo shovel got jammed on a rock? We can do a lot remotely, but if it physically breaks, or gets stuck someplace it can't get out of, we're out of luck.

So there's a huge incentive to send the safest, most conservative robots we can. Which is great in some ways, because, you know—

Curiosity's still rolling around like a boss five years longer than it was supposed to.

Yes! But even then, because we have to be *so careful*, progress is really slow.

You know how far *Opportunity* managed to go after it landed on Mars?

A little more than forty kilometers. You know how long it would take a typical person to walk that far?

A few days. Yeah, again, I think I see where you're going with this.

One human with a shovel and a really simple laboratory could accomplish more in a week than a robot can do in a decade.

And if a human discovers something new? Figures out that instead of digging, they need to, I don't know... pick up rocks? Sift through dust?

They can just go ahead and do that. You don't need to spend years and millions of dollars building an entirely new robot.

Okay, yes! You're right. We have a ton of sciencey reasons to send people to Mars, sure.

I still think the most important thing is that people *care* about Mars! We care about figuring it out, and we care about going there.

Seriously, sometimes I feel like all the science questions are just an excuse we've come up with. We want to go because we *want to go.*

Then I guess my question would be, does it matter?

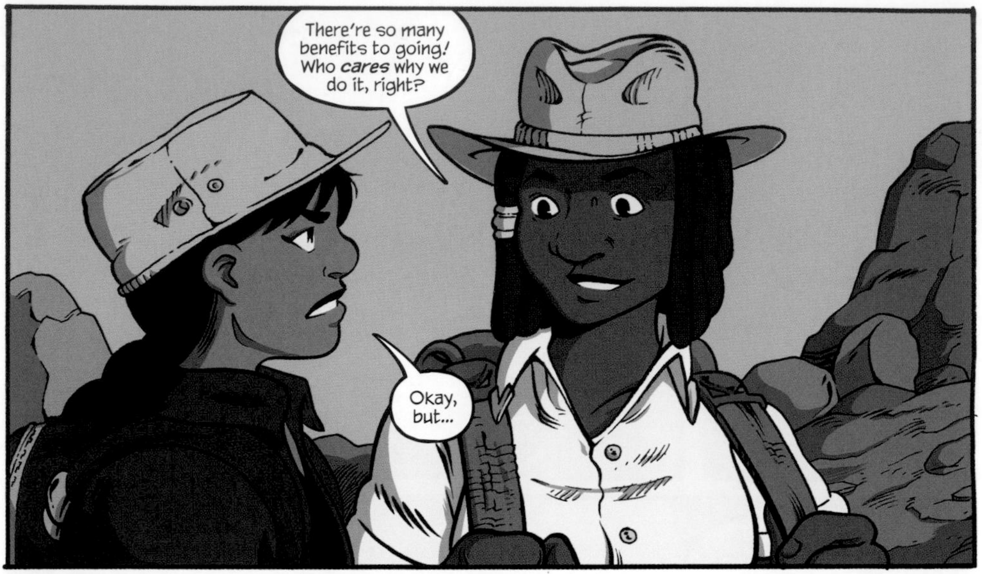
There're so many benefits to going! Who *cares* why we do it, right?
Okay, but...

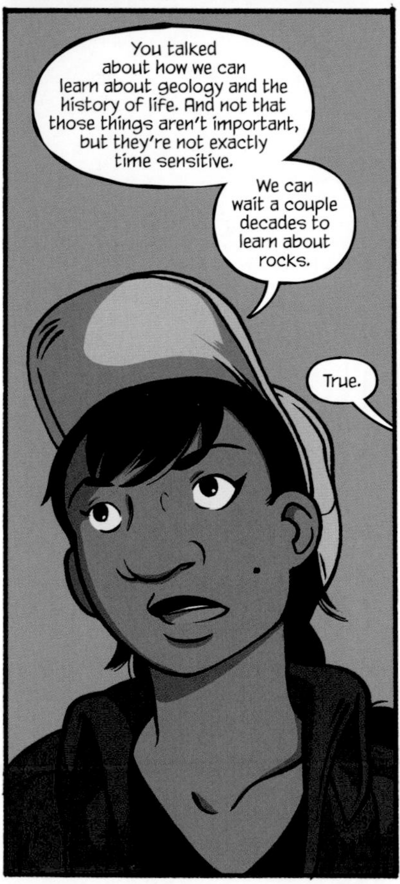
You talked about how we can learn about geology and the history of life. And not that those things aren't important, but they're not exactly time sensitive.
We can wait a couple decades to learn about rocks.
True.

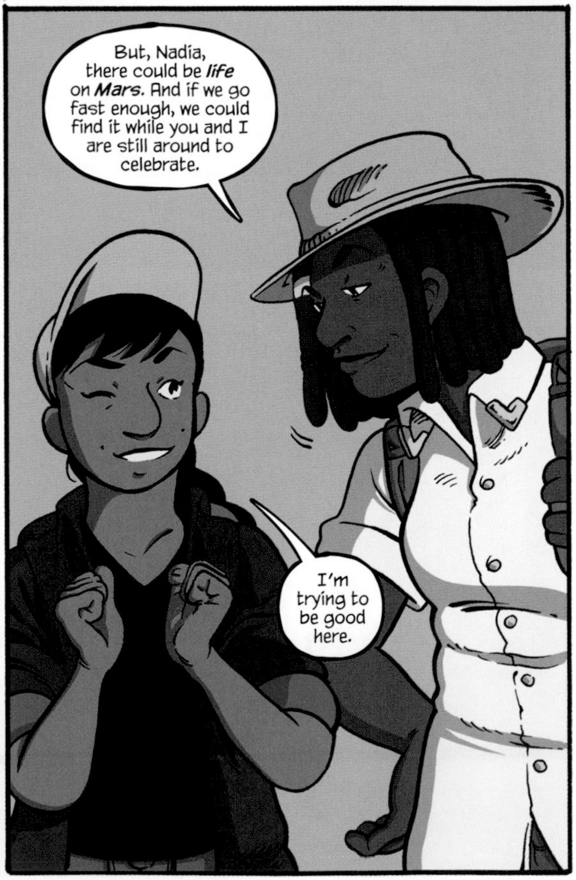
But, Nadia, there could be *life* on *Mars*. And if we go fast enough, we could find it while you and I are still around to celebrate.
I'm trying to be good here.

All right, you want pragmatic? Sure.

Space is hard. Humans in space is *really* hard, and the farther we go from Earth the harder it gets.

Getting people up into space, getting them to Mars, *landing* them on Mars, getting them *back* to Earth again, all of that stuff, it's just a huge tangle of problems that we'll need to solve.

And in the process of solving those problems, we'll discover technologies and materials and processes that we might never have figured out otherwise!

All of which are objectively good for humanity, far beyond the whole going-to-Mars issue.

Think about all the ways that going into space has made people's normal lives better!

What, like *GPS* and *MRI* machines?

And weather prediction, and crop monitoring, and water purification, and memory foam—

‹Pff›

Don't scoff at me, I'm in my thirties. I need a comfortable mattress.

Anyway, a ton of those advancements depend on our satellite system.

And we need to have a robust launch infrastructure to take care of that system and keep it working like it should.

Which isn't even getting into things like space telescopes for studying distant galaxies, or solar monitoring satellites for keeping an eye on space weather—

Space weather?

Yes!

Like if there's an eruption on the surface of the Sun—

A solar flare?

Or a coronal mass ejection. Space weather can have a *huge* impact on things like radio signals and our power grid here on Earth. And we're still learning how to monitor and predict it.

Also...look, I know we're trying not to get all science-fictiony here, but there's the whole asteroid thing...

Don't even start with the asteroid thing.

I'm just *saying.*

It'd be pretty lousy if we found out there's a giant asteroid headed for Earth but we can't do anything about it because we allowed our launch infrastructure to crumble!

All right! **All right!**

Yes, space is important! I don't know why we're even arguing about this, I agree with you!

The point is, when we send humans into space, we innovate **big-time.**

Look at how much we've learned so far, from a handful of Moon missions and some space stations in low Earth orbit, less than 500 kilometers up.

Imagine what we'd learn while trying to keep a can of humans alive all the way to Mars and back.

You make it sound so appealing...

Hey, you're the one who wants to go.

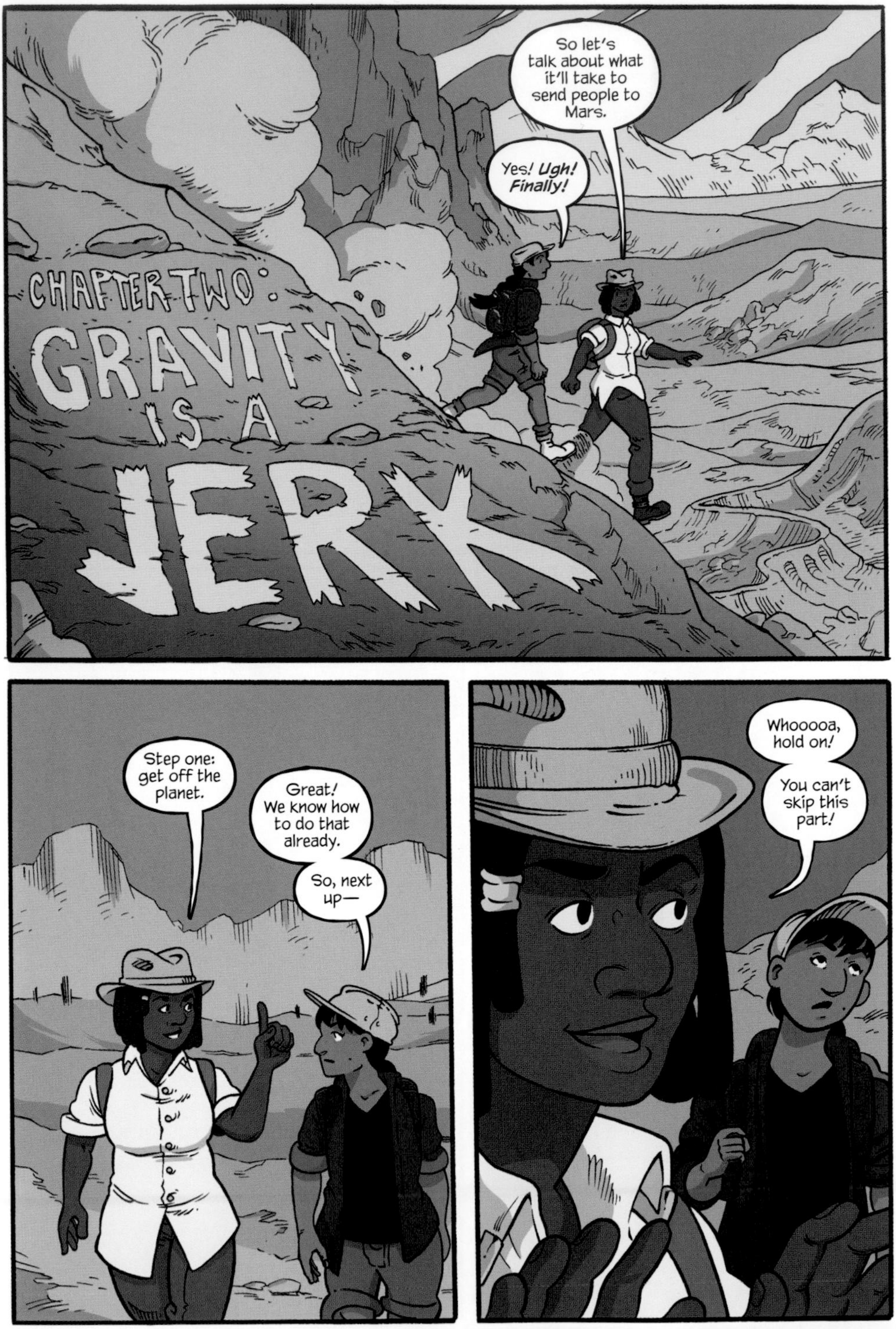

CHAPTER TWO:
GRAVITY IS A JERK
So let's talk about what it'll take to send people to Mars.
Yes! *Ugh! Finally!*
Step one: get off the planet.
Great! We know how to do that already.
So, next up—
Whoooa, hold on!
You can't skip this part!

What? We'll just use a rocket.

We've been launching things into space since, like, what, the 1950s?

1957. Sputnik.

Yeah, so like I said, we know how to do that part already.

We can know how to do a thing and still have that thing be a huge pain in the butt. I hate to be the bearer of bad news, but in a lot of ways, gravity is the number one problem holding back the space program right now.

Har har.

I'm serious!

Gravity is why it's so expensive to launch stuff into space.

Sure, but we still launch stuff into space all the time.

We launch stuff into *low Earth orbit* all the time.

There's a reason that no astronauts have left low Earth orbit since the last time we went to the Moon.

There's a reason we built the International Space Station only 400 kilometers up.

You and me, standing on the surface of the Earth right now? We're at the bottom of a well.

And it's really, *really* hard to get anything up out of it.

When you say "well" you mean like "Little Timmy's fallen to the bottom of the well!" well?

That's not the worst mental image to have, actually.

Time to visualize the invisible forces of the universe!

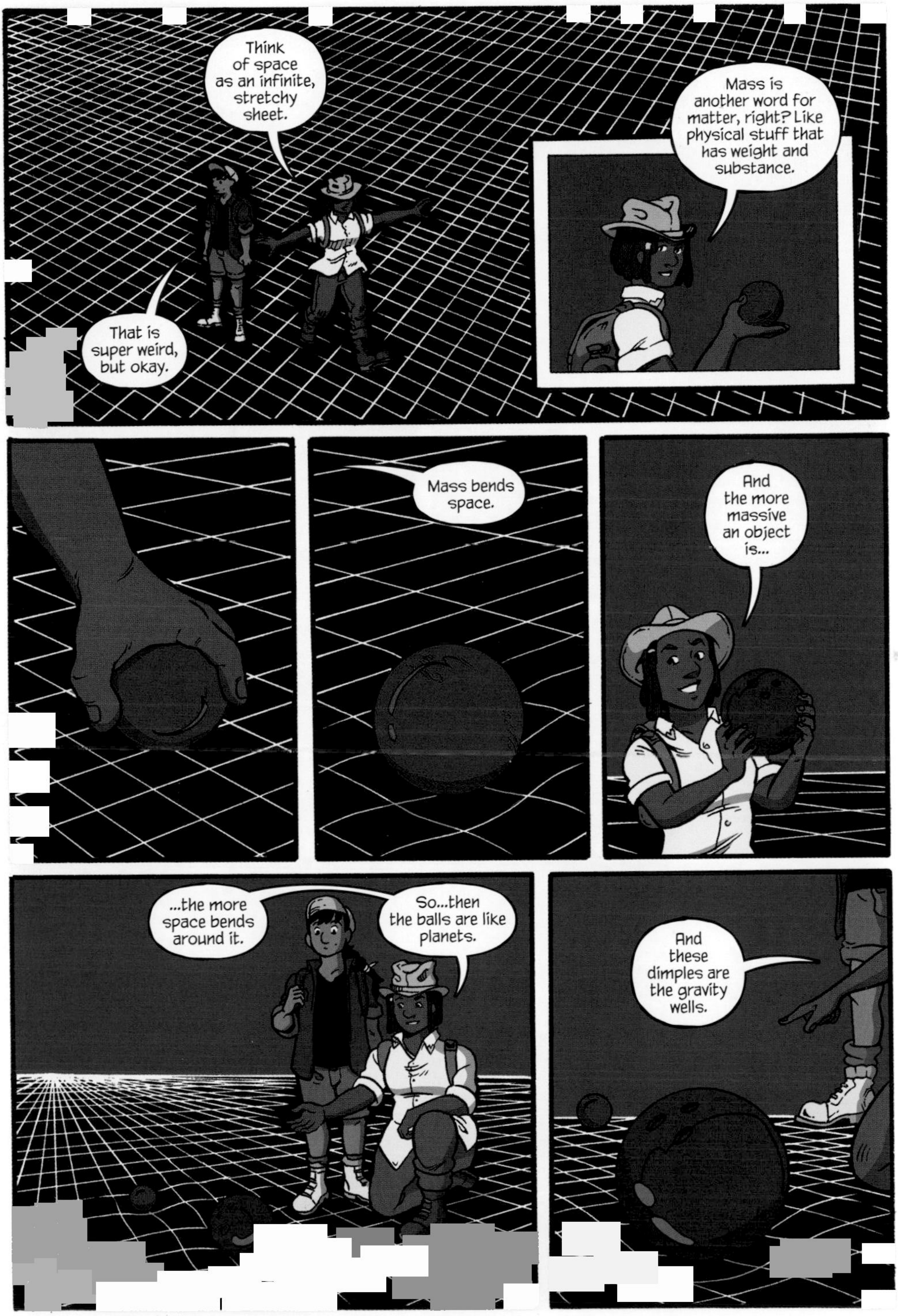
Think of space as an infinite, stretchy sheet.
That is super weird, but okay.
Mass is another word for matter, right? Like physical stuff that has weight and substance.
Mass bends space.
And the more massive an object is...
...the more space bends around it.
So...then the balls are like planets.
And these dimples are the gravity wells.

The Sun is huge, so it makes an impression in space-time that's so large and so deep, the whole rest of the solar system's caught inside it.

And all the planets...

...are spinning around the Sun in their orbits.

They're going fast enough—or to be more precise, they have enough velocity—to avoid being sucked into the center of the Sun.

But they can't break out of the solar gravity well.

You see?

The Earth's gravity well doesn't look that deep to me.

Well, not compared to the Sun, sure. But it's deep enough to keep the Moon in orbit.

And it's absolutely deep enough to cause us some serious logistical problems.

I'm not an idiot. I know we need rockets to get into space. But like I said, this is a solved problem. We launch things all the time.
You just need a big enough rocket and you're fine.
Ah, but that's the thing!
That's the whole problem!
????
$\Delta v = V_e \ln \frac{m_o}{m_f}$
Let me introduce you to the archnemesis of space exploration...
...the *rocket equation!*
$\Delta v = V_e \ln \frac{m_o}{m_f}$
Explain to me why my archnemesis is math.
$\Delta v = V_e \ln \frac{m_o}{m_f}$

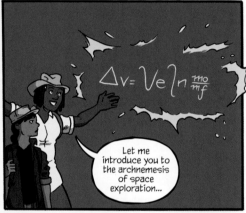

Okay, so, practically speaking, you use this equation to figure out how much fuel you'll need to launch a rocket and its payload—the thing the rocket is actually carrying.

It doesn't account for all the ticky-tack details like aerodynamics, but it's a good ballpark estimate.

$$\Delta v = V_e \ln \frac{m_0}{m_f}$$

Like any equation, it has variables. In this case, those variables are...

delta-v,

specific impulse,

and propellant mass fraction.

$$\Delta v = V_e \ln \frac{m_0}{m_f}$$

The what now?

Delta-v is short for "delta velocity," which we measure in kilometers per second.

It's the total change in velocity, which basically tells you how much effort it'll take to change from where you start to where you want to end up—to move from one trajectory to another.

So, like, going from the trajectory of sitting on a launch pad on the ground...

$$\Delta v = 8 \ km/s$$

...to the trajectory of circling the planet in low Earth orbit.

Like here, the rocket went from being at rest on the ground to traveling at eight kilometers per second relative to Earth. So that's a delta-v of eight kilometers per second!

Why don't you call it, like, "change in position"?

Keep in mind that everything on Earth is moving all of the time—the planet's turning, and the Earth orbits the Sun, and the Sun orbits the galactic core, and—

I get it and also this is making me nauseous to think about.

In normal life, that stuff doesn't matter, but when you're going up into space, you know...it matters a *lot*.

Okay. Great. Delta-v, change in trajectory. Got it. Continue.

Specific impulse is basically the amount of energy you're getting from every unit of fuel you burn. It's describing how powerful the vehicle is, based on the kind of propellant you're using.

So, like, rocket fuel has a higher specific impulse than, say, corn oil. You'll get more bang from a gallon of the first than a gallon of the second.

Sure.

And then there's the propellant mass fraction.

The mass of the fully fueled, ready-to-launch rocket goes on top. The mass of the empty rocket goes on the bottom.

Gotta be honest, this all sounds pretty reasonable.

$$\Delta v = Ve \ln \frac{mo}{mf}$$

It does, doesn't it? But I'll tell you what.

This equation is a first-class jerk.

$$\Delta v = Ve \ln \frac{mo}{mf}$$

It's...an equation.

Here, this'll help...

There.

Hey, Rocket Equation, can we go to Mars?

Depends.

If you actually start plugging numbers into this guy, here's what happens: the bigger the thing you're trying to launch into space, the more fuel you'll need.

Well, uh... of course?

Hang on! But!

That fuel is also a thing—it also has mass! So part of the fuel in your rocket is going to be burned in order to launch the weight of *other* fuel.

So you need *more* fuel to launch the fuel you need to launch the payload.

Oh...oh, no, I think I see where this is going...

If you want to launch a bigger thing—a larger satellite, a vehicle more people can sit in, whatever...

...you'll need *more* fuel...

...but then you also need *more* fuel to launch the fuel that's launching that larger payload.

Plus the actual structure of the rocket itself is getting larger and larger, too, in order to hold all of that fuel!

It just goes on and on in this endless spiral, the upshot of which...

...is an exponentially increasing mass of fuel.

Yikes.

And if you push it far enough...

...the equation breaks, and it's physically impossible to get your rocket into orbit.

But even before you reach that point, jeez, it just gets *expensive!* Humans are fragile. We need a lot of *stuff* to stay alive in space.

And launching a lot of stuff...

Means a really big rocket.

As of this moment, the largest kind of rocket that's ever been launched is the Saturn V.

That's what they used for the Apollo program.

Oh, yeah! The Moon missions!

Yes!

This rocket sent humans farther from Earth than anyone's been since, along with everything they needed to stay alive, land on the Moon's surface, and do some basic science.

So just to give you a sense of scale here, all of this made up the payload for Apollo 11—

That's the first actual Moon landing mission, right? The one with Buzz Aldrin and Neil Armstrong.

And Michael Collins, the guy stuck sitting in orbit while they moonwalked, yeah!

Here's the service module, the command module, and the lunar module. These three babies, plus the stuff that was in them, weighed about 43.9 metric tons altogether.

That's some tons.

service module

command module

lunar module

UNITED STATES

And the empty Saturn V rocket weighs 391 metric tons.

Okay, I take it back, *that* is some tons.

Ha ha, *well!* So the actual weight on the launch pad? Including all of the fuel?

2,800 metric tons.

Wait, that's like... hang on...

That freakin' rocket was 85% fuel! And almost all of that fuel was burned in order to launch the fuel that hadn't been burned yet!

It's completely bonkers when you think about it!

Astronaut Don Pettit calls the rocket equation a "tyrant" and that seems pretty apt to me.

Hooollllld up. Okay, I think I just figured something out. Is this business why we have multi-stage rockets?

Like... because when you're done using one part, you may as well dump it rather than keep burning fuel to, like...keep launching it? More?

Yes! That's it exactly!

The specifics change from one rocket to another, but the math we just talked about is why most rockets are actually made up of several smaller rockets that're all connected together.

Third Stage: S-IVB
· One J-2 engine
· Fired twice: once to reach Earth orbit, and once to set it on a trajectory toward the Moon

Second Stage: S-II
· Five Rocketdyne F-1 engines
· Fired for 384 seconds in the upper atmosphere

First Stage: S-IC
· Five Rocketdyne F-1 engines
· Fired during launch for 168 seconds
· Shut off at an altitude of 93 km

We call them stages. Every stage has its own engine, and once all the fuel in that stage is used up, it's jettisoned so that the rocket doesn't weigh as much from that point onward.

You end up having to launch with less fuel that way.

Great, well, thanks for the rocket talk. All very cool.

So all we have to do is build something that can take us to Mars, stick it on a Saturn V, and get this party started, right?

There is...a lot to unpack in that sentence.

But just to start, we can't stick *anything* on a Saturn V.

Why not?

Because there aren't any Saturn Vs *left*. Not that can fly, anyway.

We haven't launched a Saturn V rocket since 1973.

Huh...well... okay.

But we built the space station a lot more recently than that, right?

Most of the big ISS pieces were launched with the space shuttles, which NASA retired in 2011.

Space Shuttle 1981–2011

And it wouldn't have been big enough for a crewed Mars mission anyway.

I went to a space shuttle launch when I was a kid. They're *huge.*

They *are... but...*

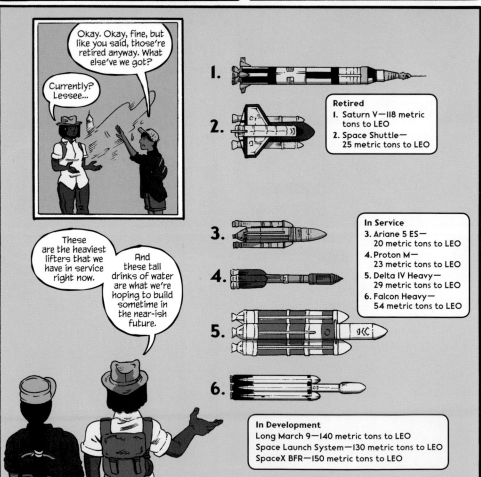

Retired
1. Saturn V—118 metric tons to LEO
2. Space Shuttle—25 metric tons to LEO

In Service
3. Ariane 5 ES—20 metric tons to LEO
4. Proton M—23 metric tons to LEO
5. Delta IV Heavy—29 metric tons to LEO
6. Falcon Heavy—54 metric tons to LEO

In Development
Long March 9—140 metric tons to LEO
Space Launch System—130 metric tons to LEO
SpaceX BFR—150 metric tons to LEO

If we're going to send people to Mars and get them home again, we'll need to launch a *lot* of stuff. Literal *tons and tons* of stuff, way more than we needed to send three dudes to the Moon for a week or two.

They spent a *week* on the Moon?

Technically they spent, like, max three days on the actual Moon, but there's going there and coming back, too...

Look, I'm simplifying!

'kay.

Point is, we don't have anything large enough to launch that much stuff all at once! Heck, I don't know if it's even physically possible.

Which means we're gonna have to send it all up in pieces and put it together in space.

Like the space station.

Exactly.

And not everyone agrees on the best way to do this!

Some people want to keep it to as few launches as possible—less opportunity for something to go wrong, bigger pieces that take less time and work to put together in space.

Other folks think we should do lots of smaller launches—we could use the rockets we already have, a problem with any one launch puts a smaller percentage of the total stuff at risk, and it might be less expensive.

Of course, it's not just the mass of the stuff that's an issue, it also matters how big it is.

Like what if you think your heat shield will need to be ten meters wide, but the largest rocket you've got can only launch something five meters wide into space?

Whoops.

Then you have to decide, how important is it to have a wide heat shield? Important enough to build a giant new rocket?

I had no idea rockets were such a pain.

So cool, and yet so many headaches.

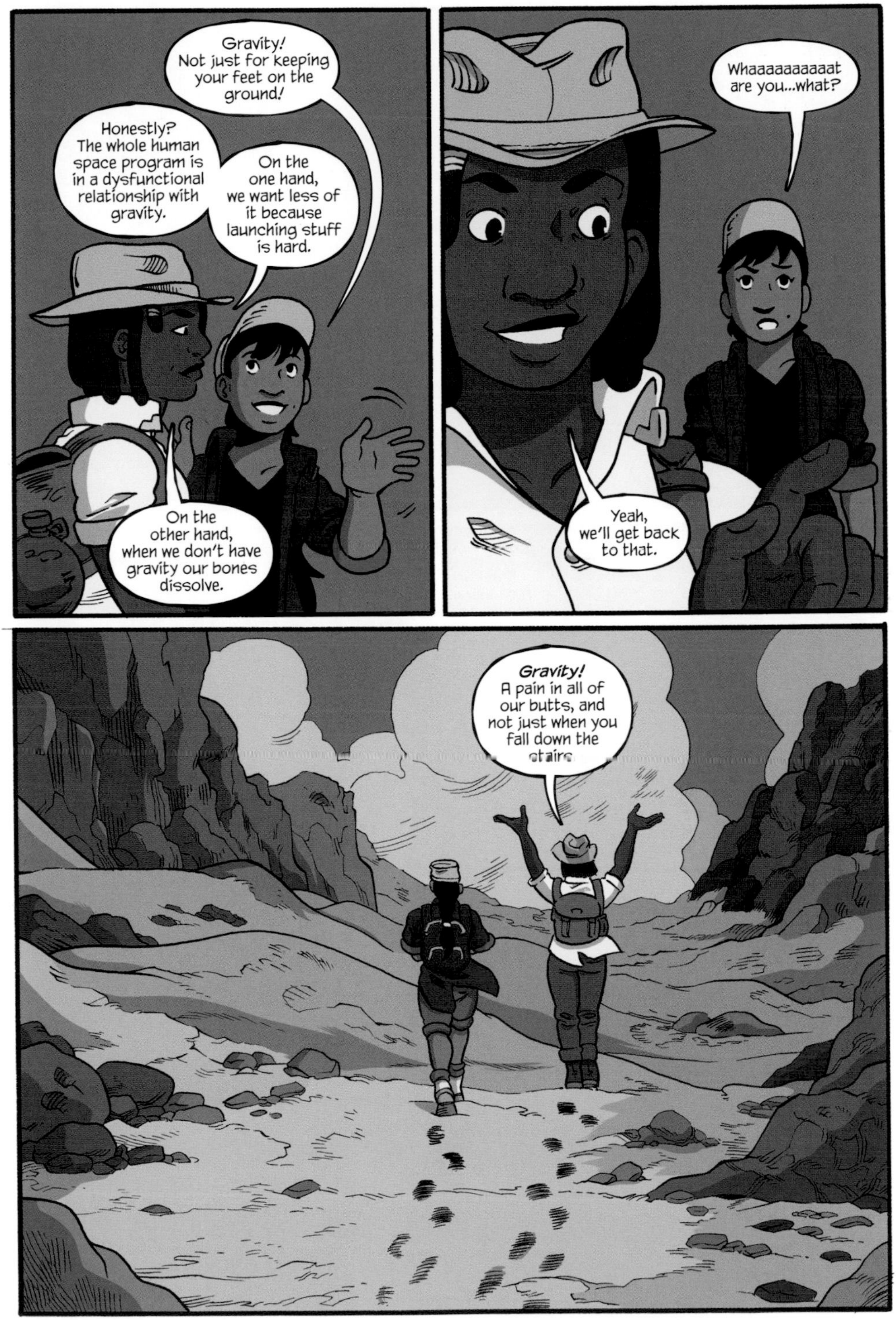
Honestly? The whole human space program is in a dysfunctional relationship with gravity.
On the one hand, we want less of it because launching stuff is hard.
On the other hand, when we don't have gravity our bones dissolve.
Gravity! Not just for keeping your feet on the ground!
Whaaaaaaaaaat are you...what?
Yeah, we'll get back to that.
Gravity! A pain in all of our butts, and not just when you fall down the stairs

All right! Okay!

I'll admit that maybe I didn't think all of this through as well as I could have.

CHAPTER THREE: A PLAN WOULD BE GOOD

Thank you for talking to me about giant rockets, much appreciated.

Happy to help.

So let's build a giant rocket and get our butts to Mars, am I right?

Well... I mean, kind of...

Eleanor.

You can't just fire a rocket at Mars whenever you feel like it—

Eleanor, you're killing me here.

Like, if you *want* to spend billions of dollars to shoot yourself at the red dot in the sky, you can go right ahead, I guess, but—

You win. Ruin my dreams.

Nadia, I am here to make your dreams come true...

...with orbital mechanics!

Okay, I'll bite. Lay it out for me.

First big thing to remember: the solar system is constantly in motion!

The Earth and Mars are both orbiting the Sun at different speeds.

24 km/s

30 km/s

Their relative positions and the distance between them varies a *lot* over time.

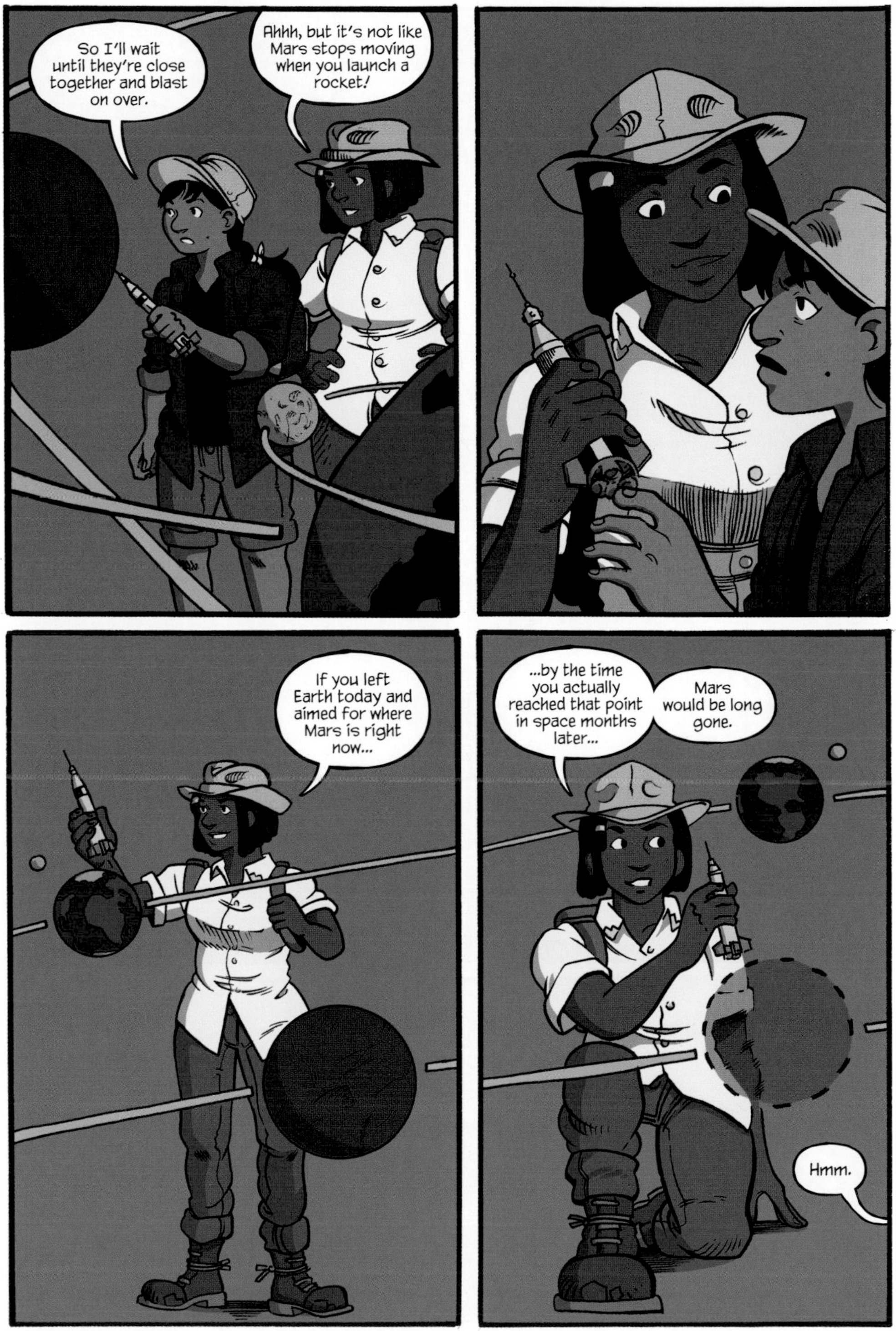
So I'll wait until they're close together and blast on over.
Ahhh, but it's not like Mars stops moving when you launch a rocket!
If you left Earth today and aimed for where Mars is right now...
...by the time you actually reached that point in space months later...
Mars would be long gone.
Hmm.

So when we're trying to figure out the best way to get to Mars, we have to take all of this movement into account—kind of like we're trying to jump from a car onto a speeding train. Only it's way more complicated, and if you miscalculate and miss the train, you'll starve and/or suffocate to death in space.

I'm coming around to the "make a plan" idea.

When we're talking about all the possible paths from one place to another in space, we call those paths "trajectories."

Any usable trajectory is carefully calculated to make sure that when your vehicle arrives at a particular point...

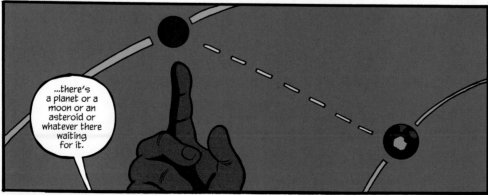

...there's a planet or a moon or an asteroid or whatever there waiting for it.

A **good** trajectory will get you to that place in the shortest time, or using the least amount of fuel—depends on what you're launching, mostly.

Past Trajectories
Venus Express: 5 months to Venus
Curiosity rover: 8 months to Mars
MESSENGER: 3 years, 5 months to Mercury

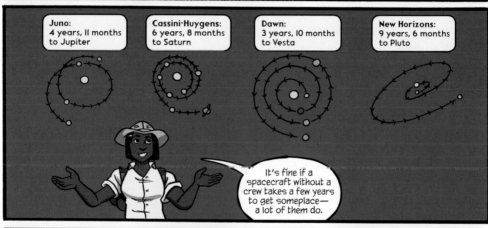

Juno:
4 years, 11 months to Jupiter

Cassini-Huygens:
6 years, 8 months to Saturn

Dawn:
3 years, 10 months to Vesta

New Horizons:
9 years, 6 months to Pluto

It's fine if a spacecraft without a crew takes a few years to get someplace—a lot of them do.

But in general it's better for humans to spend as little time in deep space as possible.

"Deep space"? We're talking about Mars. It's the next planet out in the solar system.

Anything farther away than the Moon is deep space.

You're kidding.

47

And in deep space, we have to worry a lot more than usual about space weather—the radiation, mostly. Bad space weather means your crew gets cooked.

Yikes.

Alsoooooooo there's one other thing about trajectories that makes a crewed mission way harder than the satellite and robot launches we've done so far:

We have to get them back home again.

Well... I mean, do we *really*?

I'm not helping you plan a one-way trip to Mars.

But—

Your mother would kill me.

Fine. Jeez.

So the best trajectory for sending a crew to Mars and back should use the least amount of fuel, take the shortest amount of time, have the best space weather possible, *and* allow for a safe return trip.

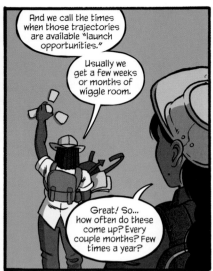

And we call the times when those trajectories are available "launch opportunities."

Usually we get a few weeks or months of wiggle room.

Great! So... how often do these come up? Every couple months? Few times a year?

Well, low-energy trajectories for sending satellites and rovers and such happen every couple of years.

I can feel a big "but" coming...

But, the good-for-humans launch opportunities are, ah...

less frequent.

Fortunately there's a pretty predictable cycle to these things—the synodic cycle, if you're curious—

I wasn't.

And it's, um...

It's fifteen years long.

Are you... wait, are you *joking*?

Nope.

We get a decent launch window for sending people to Mars every *fifteen years*? *One-five*?

Yep.

CLAP

And the next one is in 2032.

I guess we may as well get started.

Oh, absolutely, there is a *ton* of stuff to do—

POP

Like building space-ships?

Like making a bunch of decisions about how those ships are gonna work.

CHAPTER FOUR: GET TO MARS

I don't really get what the mystery is here. We'll have to send a ton of stuff to Mars, the rocket equation is a jerk, so we can't send it all up at once, so we'll use a lot of smaller rockets instead.

Like, that bites, but it sounds pretty straightforward.

Launching stuff is just step one. Once it's off of Earth, we still have to get it the rest of the way to Mars.

We've already sent a rover the size of a car to Mars, how'd we do *that*?

You mean *Curiosity*?

We packaged the rover up with a cruise stage, along with the stuff it would need to land safely on Mars, and then we launched that payload on top of an Atlas V rocket.

That launch gave it basically all of the delta-v it needed—you know, the acceleration—to get all the way to Mars.

The "cruise stage" for a vehicle like that—the part that it rides through all the open space between Earth and Mars—has little hydrazine engines that it uses for course corrections.

But those are only there to make sure the spacecraft hits the Martian atmosphere the right way—they aren't actually pushing the vehicle to Mars.

The rocket launch on Earth was big enough to push *Curiosity all the way* to another planet?

Yep.

And we can't do that to send humans to Mars because...?

Well. The whole MSL *Curiosity* package only weighed 3.8 metric tons altogether.

Hmm. And you said the Moon landings were more like fifty, right?

Yeah. And those were...

Tiny compared to what we'd need for Mars. Yeah, I remember. Hmm.

Which means that we'll need powerful onboard propulsion systems that work in deep space.

You make it sound like this is going to be a problem.

VZZ

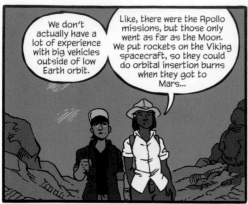

We don't actually have a lot of experience with big vehicles outside of low Earth orbit.

Like, there were the Apollo missions, but those only went as far as the Moon. We put rockets on the Viking spacecraft, so they could do orbital insertion burns when they got to Mars...

They did the what now?

Sorry, "orbital insertion burn" is basically just... "fire your engine to slow yourself down so you can enter orbit."

Great. Okay. But...

Viking? Like the Mars missions from the seventies?

Like I said, we don't do this very often.

Huh. What else you got?

Let's see...

There've been a couple of ion thruster experiments?

Ion thrusters sound good!

They are! And they worked great! But!

Deep Space 1—373 kg

Dawn—1,240 kg

The spacecraft were...pretty small.

I've had cars bigger than this. What the...

Eleanor, this is the best you've got? Are you kidding me?

It's complicated.

So let's just back up for a second and take a look at the problem.

We want to send people and cargo to Mars.

LOW THRUST   HIGH THRUST

Right now, we have four basic types of engines we think we could use for Mars transit.

FLIGHT HERITAGE

NO HE

We could honestly stand around for hours just talking about propulsion systems, but I'll stick to the two big factors that're the most important when we're planning a Mars mission: how much thrust the engine generates, and what its flight heritage is.

Flight heritage...?

That's a way to describe how much we've actually used the thing in the real world.

Nuclear thermal engines have zero flight heritage because no one's actually put one up into space.

Chemical rockets have a ton of flight heritage, because we've been using them regularly for almost a century.

It's a handy term— you can use it to talk about basically anything you ever fly into space.

So I can say that Sunita Williams has a lot of flight heritage because she's spent, like, 300 days in orbit?

Hah! Sure.

Nice.

Anyway! Types of engines!

I'll talk about the "low thrust" options first.

These are basically two different ways of powering the same engine.

They use electricity to ionize a propellant—usually an inert gas, like xenon—and accelerate those ions out the back of the engine.

That pushes the vehicle in the opposite direction, just...very, very gradually.

Oh! So these are the ion thrusters.

Yes.

Cool. Continue.

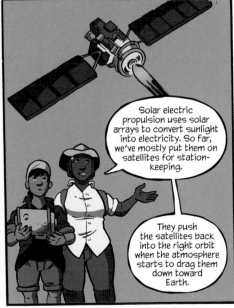

Solar electric propulsion uses solar arrays to convert sunlight into electricity. So far, we've mostly put them on satellites for station-keeping.

They push the satellites back into the right orbit when the atmosphere starts to drag them down toward Earth.

But we've made some big improvements with solar arrays in the last decade or so, and now lots of folks think this kind of system could work well on larger spacecraft, too.

For one thing, they're really efficient.

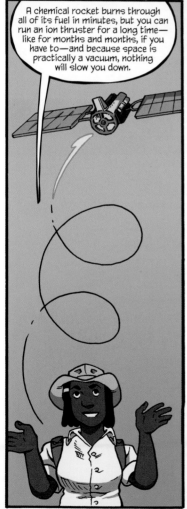

A chemical rocket burns through all of its fuel in minutes, but you can run an ion thruster for a long time—like for months and months, if you have to—and because space is practically a vacuum, nothing will slow you down.

They aren't powerful enough to punch right out of a gravity well like a rocket can...

...but once you've launched them into low Earth orbit, they can gradually climb the rest of the way out—a little like rolling up a ramp.

If they accelerate for long enough, they can build up the velocity they need to spiral up out of Earth's gravity well, cruise for a year or so...

...then turn around and slow the thing back down again so they can spiral in as they decelerate down toward Mars.

Not so great for people, but maybe okay for their luggage.

What?

You are pretty conspicuously not saying anything about the nuclear version, which sounds like it would be way more badass due to being *nuclear*.

Yeeeaaaah, well, nuclear electric propulsion **would** work really well, in theory.

Solar power gets tricky the farther you are from the Sun, **and** the solar arrays are large and add a lot of weight to your vehicle, **and** you have to worry about keeping them faced toward the Sun.

A nuclear electric engine would solve a bunch of those problems!

NUCLEAR THERMAL

But, ah... well, we've never actually flown one.

What, like not even a test run?

Not in space, no.

We've built a handful of proof-of-concept engine experiments, but those projects were all canceled back in the seventies.

But there's the other nuke engine, right? What about that?

Nuclear *thermal* propulsion would be pretty straightforward, actually.

You'd use a small reactor to heat up an inert propellant like liquid hydrogen.

As the fuel heats up, it expands, and the engine forces it out of a rocket nozzle. Thrust!

That sounds great.

Yes, it does.

Space nerds love to talk about this one. It can get you moving real fast real quick, it's efficient, the system as a whole is pretty low mass...

But?

Well, it's like I said. Nuclear thermal has absolutely no flight heritage whatsoever.

NO FLIGHT HERITAGE

Why are you even telling me about this?

Why do you dangle awesome space nukes in front of me, just to snatch them away again?

Look, I'm just reporting the conversation to you, okay? I'm laying out all the options that spaceflight people talk about, for better or worse.

If you want to join in on making Mars plans, you have to know this stuff.

Fine.

HERIT

CHEM PROPUL

So. Chemical propulsion? Is that like the chemical rockets you were talking about before?

Yep.

All right. Lay it out for me.

Well! Chemical propulsion is a pretty big umbrella, actually.

It covers almost all of the space vehicles you'd have heard of.

Definitely everything that's ever carried a human into space.

The basic idea is you use a chemical reaction to produce thrust. A Soyuz-2, like this one, is a chemical rocket.

Its stages burn kerosene, with liquid oxygen as the oxidizer.

Because rockets like this include all of the chemicals needed for combustion, their engines can keep on burning even once they leave the atmosphere.

And so can other, smaller kinds of chemical propulsion, like the hydrazine engines we use to steer rovers on their way to Mars.

The good thing about chemical propulsion is that it has a *ton* of flight heritage.

But like I said, we haven't used big rockets out in anything like open space since Apollo. And out in *deep* space, we're gonna have problems that don't turn up in the kinds of rocket launches we use to get up off of Earth.

Just to start, liquid oxygen and liquid hydrogen, which we use in most modern chemical rockets, are both cryogenic propellants.

They have to be stored at really low temperatures, like about -250°C low, in order to *stay* liquid.

But space is really cold, right?

Not...really. Not always.

If the Sun is hitting your spacecraft, it'll heat up just like it would on Earth.

And there isn't any *air* in space to help carry heat away.

So if a chemical reaction is warming up your engine, it's difficult to cool it down again.

So not only would you have to haul all that propellant out into space, you'd also have to bring along the equipment to keep it cold for all the years you're away from Earth.

Plus, those fuels are dangerous! One spark at the wrong time...

Well, what did they use for Apollo?

Monomethyl-hydrazine, with nitrogen tetroxide as an oxidizer.

Eleanor. Come on.

It's a kind of hydrazine engine. There's no air in space, so no oxygen. You need an oxidizer to burn fuel.

Better. Continue.

Hydrazine's handy— it stays liquid at convenient temperatures and has a high freezing point, so as long as the spacecraft keeps it warm, it's fine.

But hydrazine is also really unstable! And toxic!

Super toxic, actually, real bad news, and lots of folks are pushing for spacecraft to stop using it.

You can't poison space, can you?

No, but you can poison the people who fuel up the vehicle.

Fair.

So all kinds of propulsion are garbage? Like...that's what you're saying, right?

Oh! No, not at all!

It's just that a Mars mission is a complicated problem, and no one kind of propulsion will be perfect for every type of vehicle.

I'm just laying out the options.

Great, so tell me which ones are the best and let's move on.

Well, it's not like any of them are *objectively* the best...

In your personal opinion, then.

The landscape of propulsion is changing all the time...but if I *had* to pick engines to use *right now*...

You do.

Well...

I'd say we should send the cargo out ahead of time with solar electric ion engines.

And we should figure out a chemical propulsion system that'll work in deep space, and use that for the crew.

What?

I guess... I don't get why we aren't sending all of the Mars stuff together.

Like...

Wouldn't this be easier? I get that we have to break things down into a bunch of launches, but once it's all up in space, why don't we put a big ship together, load it with the stuff we need...

...and head to Mars all in one go?

Well, we *might* end up doing it that way. But sending cargo and equipment ahead of time has some advantages.

We could have fuel-generating plants and a habitat and water collectors all set up and waiting for the crew before they even launch from Earth.

And that way, if there's a problem...

we can cancel or push back when the crew leaves.

You mean, we can make sure their Mars camp is all set up before we send them there to live in it.

Yes!

And since equipment and cargo handle being in space a *lot* better than people do, we can take our time and use a cheaper, more efficient kind of propulsion to send it.

Like solar electric.

And then we can use the faster, more powerful chemical engines for the crew.

And then it's like I said, right? Slap a spaceship together in orbit and burn our way to Mars, heck yeah.

Well...

What? *What?*

I mean, we *could* assemble the transit vehicle in low Earth orbit, if we wanna have our butts handed to us by the rocket equation.

What're you talking about? We'd already be off Earth, right?

Sure...

...but low Earth orbit is still pretty far down the gravity well.

It would take a *lot* of energy to push a transit vehicle the rest of the way out.

So, what, we build it out here? We're going full Moon Base?

Some folks want to park the whole assembly operation at an Earth-Moon Lagrangian point.

WHAP!

Which are...

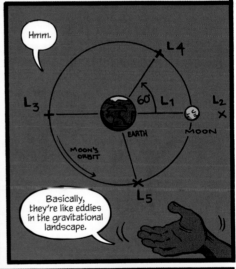

Hmm.

L4
L3
L1
L2
MOON
EARTH
60°
MOON'S ORBIT
L5

Basically, they're like eddies in the gravitational landscape.

L4

ZOOP!

The upshot is that if you put something at one of these points in space, it'll stay there without a lot of help.

L4

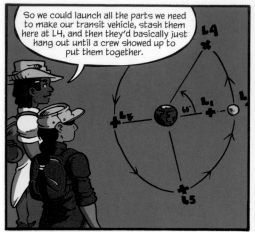

So we could launch all the parts we need to make our transit vehicle, stash them here at L4, and then they'd basically just hang out until a crew showed up to put them together.

Once the vehicle's all set and the crew's on board, it could fire its engines and be on its way to Mars.

Hang on, how far away are these Lagrangian things? Because this looks pretty far.

The really stable ones are on the orbital path of the Moon.

So, um... about 384,000 kilometers.

Look, yadda yadda rocket equation, but for real, wouldn't it be way easier to put something together, like...

...I don't know, close to the space station? Where all the potential ship-assembling astronauts live?

Well, there're advantages to doing this stuff close to home, and advantages to doing it farther away.

70

Ellie, this all seems *wicked* hard. And vague? Like... jeez, what are we even talking about? Like, physically?

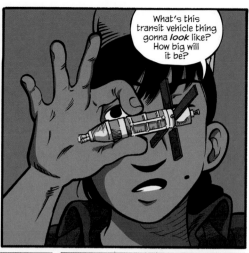

What's this transit vehicle thing gonna *look* like? How big will it be?

Will we build it from a bunch of different modules, like the space station? Will it have a spinny part for centrifugal gravity?

Or will it just be a can with an engine on the back of it?

Honestly? I don't know.

We have ideas. *Lots* of ideas. But the specifics will depend on so many things!

What technology is available? How many people are we sending? How long will their trip to Mars take? How much money do we have to spend?

But we *do* have some ideas about what a Mars transit vehicle will have to be able to do.

You know, if we want those people to actually be alive on the other end.

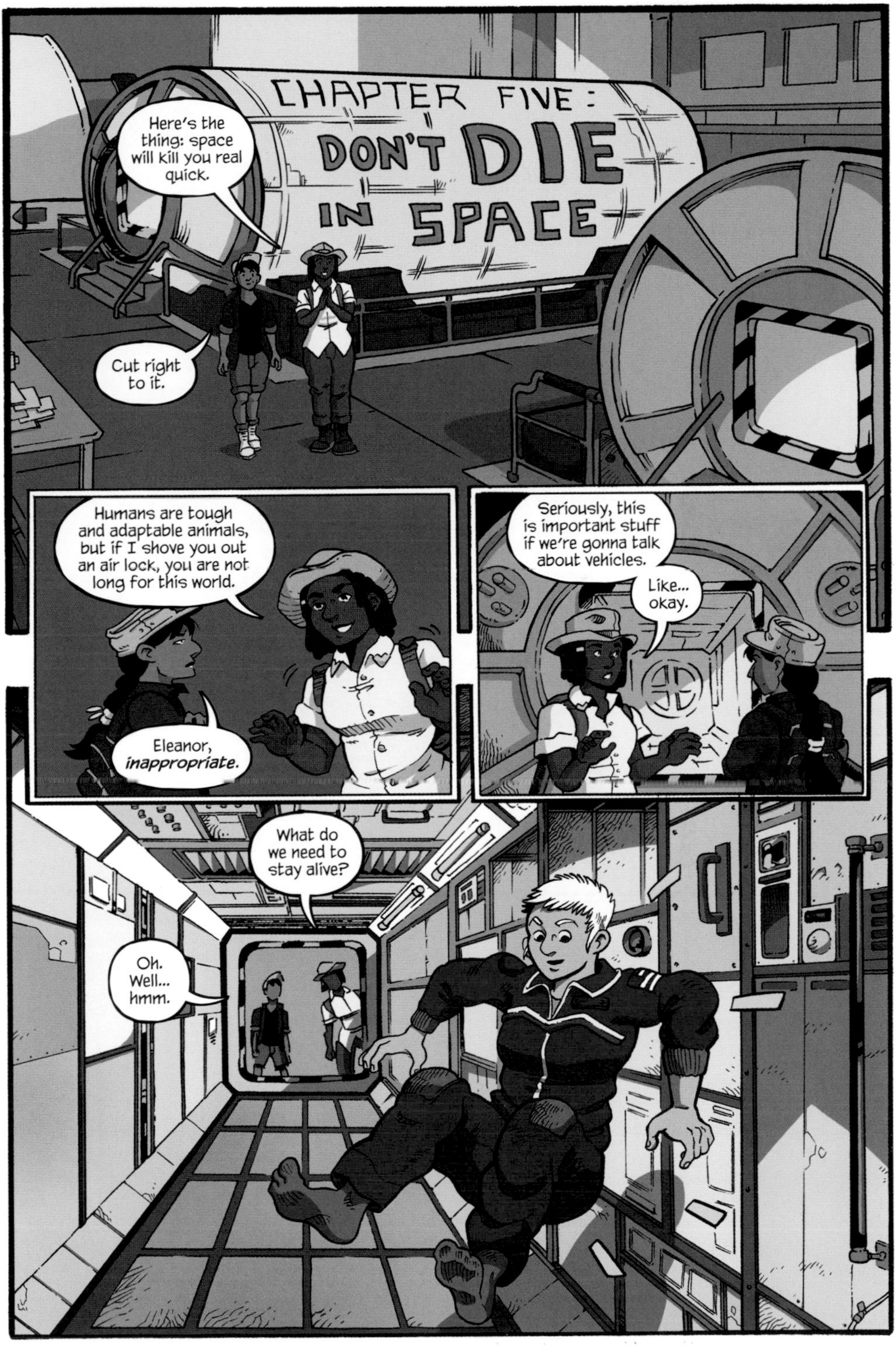
CHAPTER FIVE:
DON'T DIE IN SPACE
Here's the thing: space will kill you real quick.
Cut right to it.
Humans are tough and adaptable animals, but if I shove you out an air lock, you are not long for this world.
Eleanor, *inappropriate*.
Seriously, this is important stuff if we're gonna talk about vehicles.
Like... okay.
What do we need to stay alive?
Oh. Well... hmm.

Air. Or... I guess oxygen?

And we need the air pressure to be high enough for water to be liquid, and for all the oxygen that's already in our blood to stay there.

Wait, what?

Well, water boils when the energy of its molecules is too great for air pressure to keep them from flying away from one another.

Like in your kitchen, you use heat to add more energy to the water and bring it to a boil.

But if there's no air pressure, even at room temperature there's nothing to stop liquid water from just flying apart into a gas.

Now, your *blood* won't boil if you're in vacuum, because the rest of your body is holding it in place. *But*, without air pressure, the gases that're normally dissolved in your blood start to come out of solution, and this is *bad news*.

Your tissues stop getting oxygen, your circulation stops working properly, your lungs collapse.

It's an extreme version of the decompression sickness that happens to deep-sea divers if they head back up to the surface too quickly.

Yikes.

Okay, what else...

Food and water.

And keep in mind, we have to make sure all this stuff is clean and won't make us sick.

Yeah, let's just have a blanket "not poison" rule across the board.

Hmm. I guess we need the temperature to be in a safe range. Like, we don't want to freeze to death or to burst into flames.

No.

I guess we need to sleep?

Occasionally.

And didn't you say something about radiation a little while back? That's a big "avoid."

We absolutely do not want to get cooked by radiation, no.

MILK

75

So a ship that could take us to Mars would be a lot like the space station, right? Nice and big, can keep people alive for a long time.

A Mars transit vehicle would be similar in some ways, yes.

So haven't we figured all this stuff out? Humans have been living in orbit for *ages*.

Well... *kind of*, but...

There's no "kind of," the space station's freakin' up there right now!

Yes, but...

It's not like we could put an engine on the ISS and blast it toward Mars.

Of course not, that's stupid.

We'll build a little portable space station...

...and put an engine on *that*. And it'll be better, right? 'Cause of the whole flight heritage thing.

Well, *kind* of.

The station has flight heritage for being a station.

Its systems can't take you to another planet.

Why not?

It's had people living on it for almost twenty years.

It's not gonna take twenty years to get to Mars!

That's true, but...

Let's back up a second.

Lots of things are *way harder* in space than on Earth.

Define "lots of things."

Most things!

When there's no air pushing back against the outside of your hull, it's hard to pressurize the inside without making it explode.

It's also hard to keep the inside at a safe temperature when it's full of people and machinery—the outside gets blasted with sunlight, and when you're in a vacuum, it's hard to get rid of the heat your equipment is making.

Inside, where you're actually living, you don't have gravity pulling the cool air toward the floor...

...so you need fans to keep the atmosphere moving around. You'll have a cloud of hot carbon dioxide floating around your face when you sleep if you don't do something about it.

It's hard to move fluid around, too—just like you need fans for the air, you need pumps for your water. And for the ammonia in the radiators outside.

Jeez, everything is just *difficult*.

Fine, fine, space is hard, I get it. But we seem to be managing, right? How many people have lived on the space station? At least a hundred.

More than two hundred, actually.

And all of those people breathed air and ate food and drank water and didn't have their lungs collapse.

Sure, but...

...the space station is orders of magnitude easier to deal with than a vehicle that can take people all the way to Mars.

Why?

pft

Because people on the station are *really* close to Earth.

The space station is only about 250 miles up. When I'm sitting in my apartment in Houston and the station passes overhead, it's closer to me than I am to New Orleans.

In an emergency, station crew can jump in a Soyuz capsule and be on the ground again in three and a half hours.

Hmmm.

Plus, we are *constantly* launching consumables up to the station.

Time out! Consumables?

Literally just stuff you consume. You know, food, water, energy.

When you say "constantly launching"...

We send a resupply vehicle every month or so.

They're cargo runs, basically.

And a ton of that cargo is consumables.

Let's see...

Oxygen, water, food...plus, the station does leak a bit, so they have to send up tanks of inert gas to help keep it pressurized.

And then on top of that we have propellant, spare parts, experiments, crew care packages...

Banana?

How many people are living on the station?

Six, usually.

That is...a *lot* of launches for six people.

It is, kinda.

All right. Go ahead and tell me how screwed we are.

It's not that we're screwed, exactly.

We've just been able to get away with old ways of doing things for a long time. And if we want to go to Mars, we'll have to put some more effort into learning how to close the loop.

...The what now?

When I say "close the loop," I mean creating a more self-contained system.

The Earth is an almost completely closed loop.

Sunlight goes in, and that energy drives the engine of our entire ecosystem. The air we breathe and the water we drink and the food we eat all come from inside the envelope of atmosphere around our planet, and the same goes for every other living thing on Earth.

When we design a human-rated vehicle, we're basically just making a small, cruddy copy of the Earth that we can tote around with us in space.

And the loops are... messier.

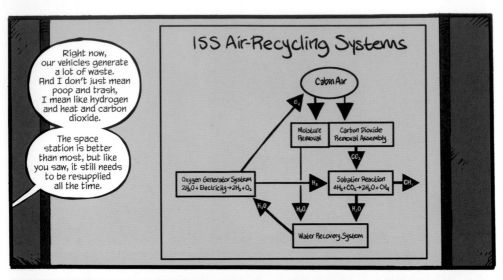

Right now, our vehicles generate a lot of waste. And I don't just mean poop and trash, I mean like hydrogen and heat and carbon dioxide.

The space station is better than most, but like you saw, it still needs to be resupplied all the time.

If we figure out ways to **use** that waste and funnel it back into the system, that's what we call closing the loop. A closed life-support loop means less stuff is getting dumped overboard or crammed into trash bags.

The more we can close the loop, the less consumable stuff we'll have to carry with us to Mars.

And that's *key*. We're gonna have to sweat every kilogram we send to Mars.

Great. Close the loop. Got it.

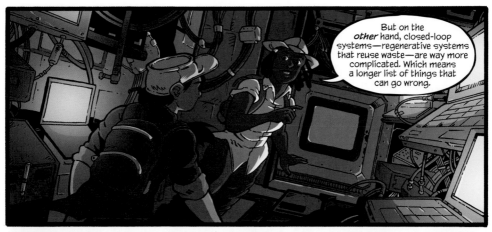

But on the *other* hand, closed-loop systems—regenerative systems that reuse waste—are way more complicated. Which means a longer list of things that can go wrong.

It takes a ton of work to keep the space station's ECLSS working right. A lot of crew time is taken up by maintenance.

Wait, "Eek-less"? Am I hearing that right?

Yes, sorry! Stands for "Environmental Control and Life Support System."

It's a blanket term for a bunch of interconnected systems, actually. These racks handle air revitalization, oxygen generation, carbon dioxide removal, water recovery, and waste management.

That last one's just the bathroom.

So all the life-support stuff happens in these machines...?

Oh, no, not at all.

The Russian segments have their own service module with its own life-support system, and plus there's a ventilation system that runs through the whole station, the fire suppression system...I'd say the radiators and the rest of the thermal control system counts...oh, also the airlock, which has its own tanks of nitrogen and oxygen...

Yeah, no, you're gonna have to explain that a little more.

These systems all have to cooperate to make sure the astronauts have fresh air to breathe at the right pressure, that the inside of the space station doesn't overheat...

...that clean water comes out when you turn on a tap, that dirty water goes where it's supposed to and gets cleaned up so we can use it again, and that the air locks work when we need them.

Better.

In a lot of ways, the space station's ECLSS is just an updated version of what we used to fly on the shuttles, but we've made some big improvements.

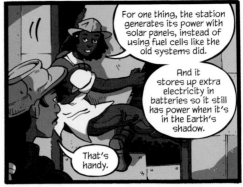

For one thing, the station generates its power with solar panels, instead of using fuel cells like the old systems did.

And it stores up extra electricity in batteries so it still has power when it's in the Earth's shadow.

That's handy.

WATER RECOVERY SYSTEM · WATER RECOVERY SYSTEM · OXYGEN GENERATOR

Then there's the water recovery system, which takes all the waste water on the station—including urine, and all the humidity it's wrung out of the air—and turns it back into something you can drink.

Plus, some of that water gets electrolyzed to make oxygen. Real handy.

Hold up...weren't you just telling me about all the water and air we're sending up to the station all the time?

Yeah, well. The station's life-support system isn't perfect, and it's full of...not holes, but dead ends?

Places where resources can't be reused.

Like, we can get a lot of the water out of human waste, but not nearly all of it. We dump a ton of hydrogen and carbon dioxide overboard, which is really too bad because we could be using them to *make* more water.

Why don't we?

Because the machine we sent up to do that—a Sabatier reactor—keeps breaking down. It's hooked into the air revitalization system, and it *should* be processing hydrogen and carbon dioxide into water and methane.

But they've had all kinds of problems with condensation inside of its mechanisms, and it's been a heck of a time figuring out why.

The *air* system on the station isn't working?

Why didn't I hear about this? That's really bad!

I mean... it's *pretty* bad.

But things on the station break down all the time.

Like we're supposed to have *two* working carbon dioxide removal system racks, for safety reasons.

Too much CO2 will poison the crew—we can't mess around with this stuff.

But the rack here in *Tranquility* was offline for ages, which meant the rack in the Destiny Lab was running without a backup.

Double yikes. Eleanor, what the heck, this is *normal?*

Well, yeah. This sort of thing is the central problem with life-support systems.

It's hard to build something on the ground and be sure it'll work in microgravity; once your machines are in space they wear down in unpredictable ways...

...and as a bonus, your life *literally* depends on them.

But, I mean, we've *mostly* got it figured out, right? Like that's the whole point of building the space station? To learn how to live in space?

And it's been in orbit since... hmmm...

Russia launched the first module in 1998.

Yes, see? We've been at this for, like, *twenty* years. Obviously if we built a brand-new life-support system now, it'd be way better!

Like, you've just walked me through why we're absolutely ready to send my butt to Mars.

UNITY

Well...

...maaaaaaaaaaaybe?

But it's a **lot** harder to send people to Mars than to keep them alive in low Earth orbit.

Why?

It's like I said. Mars is really, really, *really* far away.

Just for perspective, the farthest a human being has *ever* been from Earth is 400,171 kilometers.

The closest Mars gets to Earth is about 56,000,000 kilometers.

Apollo 13, 1970

It's just a completely different scale.

Fine. All right.

But what does that *mean*?

Like, practically speaking, why can't we just head out there with newer, better versions of the space station systems?

Let's go back to what you said before about the space station having flight heritage. You're *right*, it does, and that's especially important when it comes to life support.

Life support is wet and messy and degrades over time—corrosion, mold, water in the wrong places, buildup in hoses, pumps and valves breaking down. Slow-motion failures you can't fake in a lab.

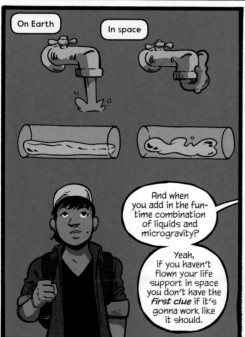

On Earth

In space

And when you add in the fun-time combination of liquids and microgravity?

Yeah, if you haven't flown your life support in space you don't have the *first clue* if it's gonna work like it should.

Sure, but we already know the space station systems work, like, we're using them right now. So what's the problem?

The problem is that a crewed Mars mission is going to be very far away from Earth for a very long time, and we've never managed both those things at once.

ISS: Canada/Japan/Russia/USA/European Space Agency—1998–present
Skylab: USA—1973–1979
Mir: USSR/Russia—1986–2001

I guess on the "long time" side we've got the space station.

Plus Skylab and *Mir*.

beep

As for "far away," there's really just the Apollo missions. Which, like you said, not actually all that far.

And they lasted for less than two weeks.

So let's start talking about the different levels of difficulty we're dealing with.

NASA came up with a way to break it down that I think is pretty handy: they classify crewed missions as "Earth Reliant," "Proving Ground," or "Earth Independent."

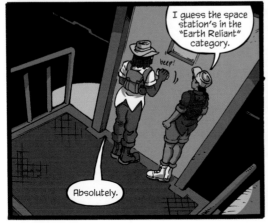

I guess the space station's in the "Earth Reliant" category.

beep!

Absolutely.

The way it's set up, the station *cannot* function without constant ground support.

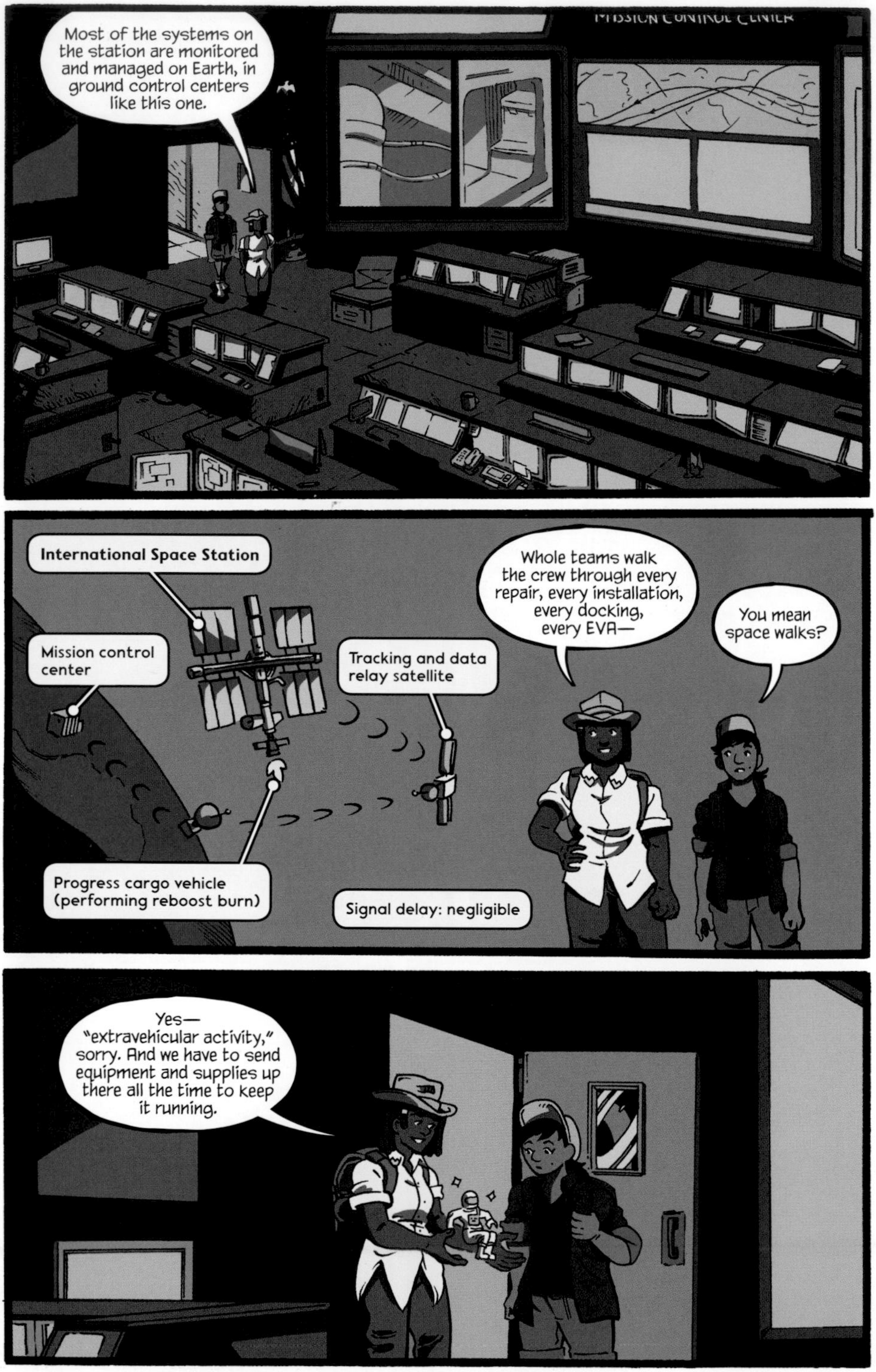
Most of the systems on the station are monitored and managed on Earth, in ground control centers like this one.
International Space Station
Mission control center
Tracking and data relay satellite
Progress cargo vehicle (performing reboost burn)
Signal delay: negligible
Whole teams walk the crew through every repair, every installation, every docking, every EVA—
You mean space walks?
Yes— "extravehicular activity," sorry. And we have to send equipment and supplies up there all the time to keep it running.

So if we stopped talking to the station or sending them more stuff, how long would it last?

Depends on when the last reboost burn happened.

That's when it gets pushed back into a higher orbit, right?

Yep. It could last without one for a few months, maybe.

After that, the station would fall into the atmosphere and break apart into fiery chunks.

Wow wow wow no.

Yeah, not ideal.

Earth-Moon L4

Deep space communications complex

Signal delay: less than two seconds

All right. What about the "Proving Ground"?

The idea is that these missions would be stepping stones to help us learn how to live and work farther away from Earth.

Conditions about Moon-distance away are more like they'd be in deep space, but the crew would still be close enough to talk to Earth without much lag, could be resupplied, and could get back home again in under a week.

So far, the Apollo missions are the only practice we've had with this.

That leaves "Earth Independent" for Mars.

Which is where we leave most of our humans-in-space experience behind.

A Mars-bound crew would have to be pretty self-sufficient.

Mars Transit Vehicle
Signal delay: four to twenty-four minutes

No resupply, so you're stuck with cargo you brought along, and whatever you can mine from the Martian air and ground.

Big lag talking to mission control, so they couldn't walk you through tricky jobs.

And even if things start to go *really* bad, there's no way to come home early.

Seriously? I know it would be *hard*, but I've seen movies where—

Movies are liars. About this, anyway.

It would take an enormous amount of fuel to change course and head back to Earth. *Way* more than you'd be able to bring.

Any vehicle you ride to Mars had better be rock-solid reliable.

But hey, let's just say we've figured all that out!

Great.

Let's say we have an amazing life-support system, runs smooth as anything, nice tight loop, the works.

Fantastic.

All of that is just, like, the *bare minimum* of staying alive.

Staying *healthy* is a whole other thing on top of that.

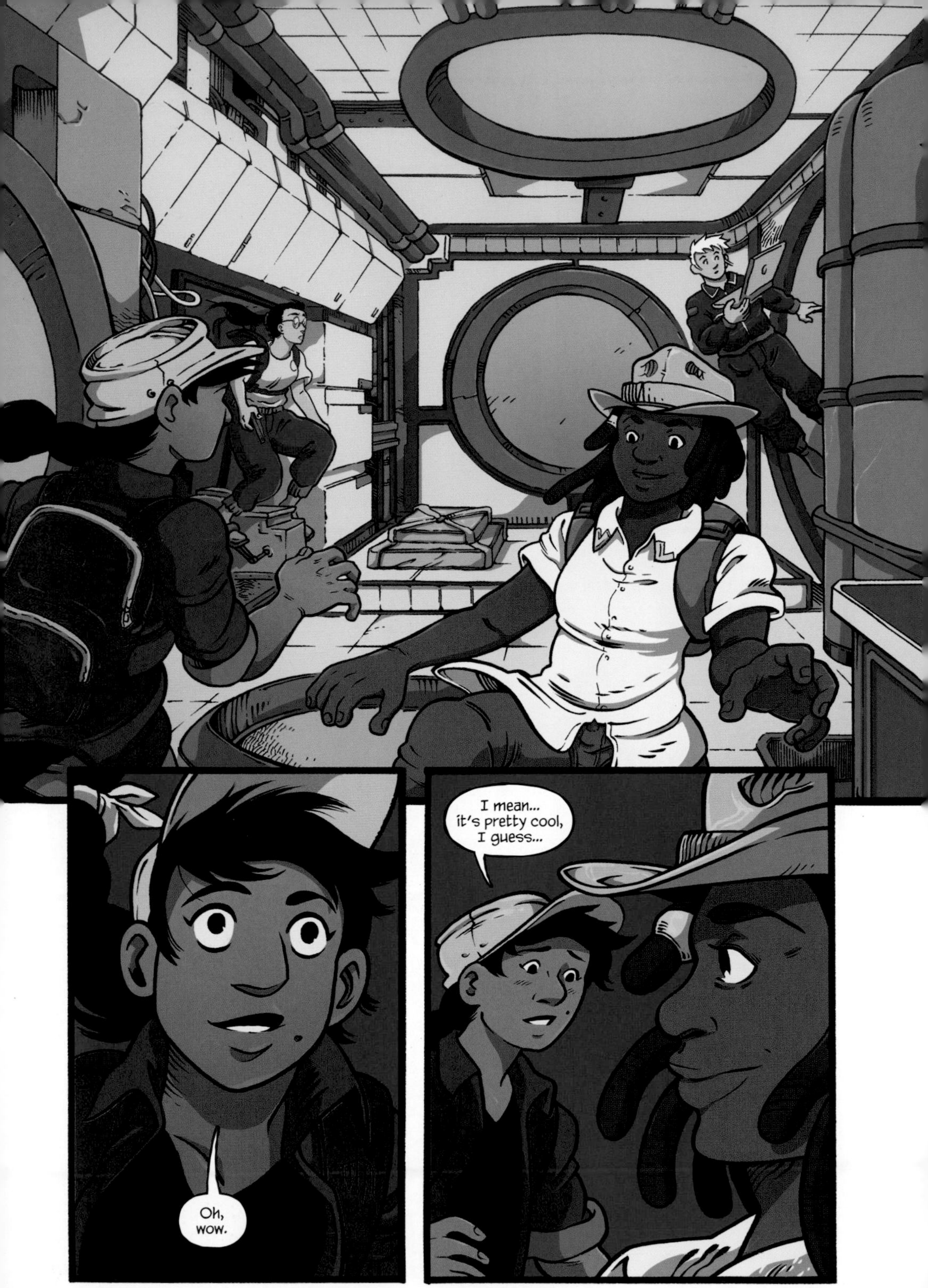
Oh, wow.
I mean... it's pretty cool, I guess...

Look, obviously we already know how to stay healthy in space.

Astronauts exercise all the time. Like two hours a day, right?

About that.

Do you know *why*?

Because they aren't using their muscles to walk around.

Welllllllll...

Go ahead.

I mean, that's *part* of it.

Ironically, the reason microgravity is so bad for us is because we're *really* good at adapting to it. Our bodies start to change almost immediately.

Without gravity pulling it downward, blood accumulates in your chest and head.

Your heart doesn't have to work against gravity, so it weakens.

The signals from your inner ear, your eyes, and your perception of your own body's movement and position all conflict with each other, causing disorientation.

Microgravity can cause a decrease in bone density, and changes in blood pressure stiffens some arteries.

Due to the extra fluid in your head, your optic nerves are compressed, the backs of eyeballs are flattened, and optic discs swell. This all affects your vision.

When we don't need our bones or muscles to support our own weight, our bodies cannibalize them and use those resources elsewhere.

And spaceflight can cause immune dysfunction.

Plus, all that extra fluid in our heads can make our faces swell up.

Okay. *Weird.*

Fortunately, we have a ton of experience with how to keep people healthy in orbit.

Many, many astronauts and cosmonauts have lived up there for months at a time.

Plus, it turns out that long-term bed rest causes a lot of the same health problems as microgravity, which lets us study them in a lab with controlled conditions and a bigger sample size.

So we know this stuff, then. We've figured it out.

We're pretty okay at microgravity damage control. But it's rough.

When astronauts come back to Earth, they don't feel great for a few days, and they need help from landing recovery crews.

And the longer they're up there, the harder the transition back to Earth can be.

For the first day or so, they need some help getting around. Their backs hurt from the strain of having to bear a human being's weight again. Their bones may be more prone to breaking.

Their balance is totally shot. They're not allowed to drive for two or three weeks because their spatial sense is all messed up.

When an astronaut comes home from orbit, they can afford to take things a little easier for the first few weeks.

When we go to Mars, though?

It's a smaller planet, but it still has gravity.

Oh...wait, I see where you're going with this. We're only gonna have so much time on the surface...

Exactly.

The whole point of this is to have human beings living and working on Mars, not lying in bed inside the habitat. But we don't want anyone to break a hip, either.

Or crash a rover.

So! We need to get better at keeping people healthy in space.

And that need is a big part of the argument for building a transit vehicle with simulated gravity.

Oh, man.

Oh, *man*, I know what this is...

A centrifuge! *Yesssss!* These things are so cool!

You know how it works, right?

Yeah, like you spin a ring-shaped module, and centrifugal force pushes everything inside of it away from the center.

So the outer side of the ring becomes a "floor" you can stand on.

Even a small centrifuge like this one, simulating just a fraction of Earth's gravity, could make a big difference for the health of the crew. A little bit of gravity is better than none!

Bonus: it would be sweet as heck.

Man, it totally would be.

All right. What other horrors of spaceflight did you want to tell me about?

Well, now I feel like a jerk—

Good. Now spit it out.

Ha ha, *well!* Radiation's a big one.

What, like from the badass nuclear engine I'm gonna put on my spaceship?

No, like from the *Sun.*

And from the mysterious depths of the galaxy!

You're messing with me.

I am *completely* serious.

Here, you'll need these.

First you have solar flares, which are basically enormous eruptions on the surface of the Sun. The movement of matter inside of the Sun can contort the Sun's magnetic fields, creating huge loops of plasma.

And when those fields snap back together...

...they send high-energy particles flying outward very, very fast.

Whoa!

We also have galactic cosmic rays, another variety of high-energy particles, although...

...we're not entirely sure where they come from? Partly supernovas? Anyway.

When you say "high-energy particles," what do you mean exactly?

I mean "ionizing radiation." As in, the *super-bad-news* kind of radiation that can kill you, or destroy your electronic equipment, or both.

Hold up. There are literal cosmic death rays shooting at us from all directions.

Yep.

All the time.

Seems like.

Okay, I must be missing something.

I guess I can see how maybe the Earth's atmosphere protects us on the ground. But if cosmic rays are so dangerous, why aren't the space station astronauts all dead?

Because in low Earth orbit, they're still tucked up in the Earth's magnetosphere. Our magnetic field deflects those high-energy particles so that most of them flow around and away from Earth instead of hitting the atmosphere, or the station.

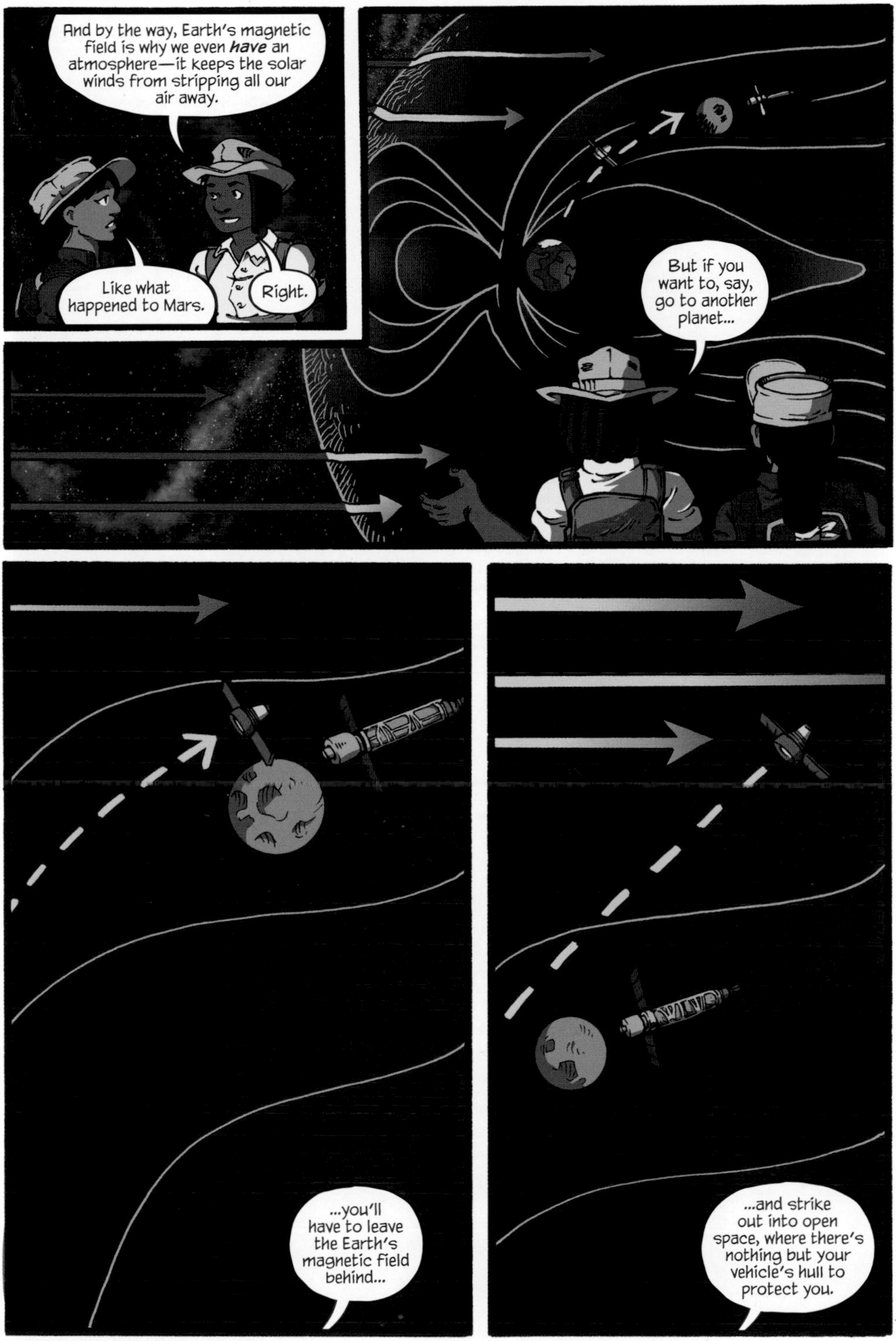
And by the way, Earth's magnetic field is why we even ***have*** an atmosphere—it keeps the solar winds from stripping all our air away.
Like what happened to Mars.
Right.
But if you want to, say, go to another planet...
...you'll have to leave the Earth's magnetic field behind...
...and strike out into open space, where there's nothing but your vehicle's hull to protect you.

25-year-old Female Career Limit = 1 Sievert

55-year-old Male Career Limit = 4 Sieverts

Just to give you an idea of the scale here, right now NASA's *lifetime* radiation dose limit for astronauts is between one and four sieverts, depending on your gender and your age.

An astronaut on the space station isn't as protected as you are when you're under Earth's thick atmosphere—they get dosed with about .075 sieverts of radiation a year.

Okay. And on the way to Mars?

More like one sievert every year, depending on what the Sun is doing. And most of our Mars mission architectures would take at least *two* years.

So...they might have to change those rules about radiation limits.

Looks like.

What's radiation even *do* to you, exactly?

Bad stuff.

Deets.

Well.

We're not completely sure.

Because we've spent so little time outside Earth's magnetic field, we don't know very much about exactly how cosmic rays will interact with our bodies. The only health effect we've seen so far in astronauts are radiation cataracts.

That's when your eyes get clouded over.

Yeah.

But we're pretty sure that chronic exposure to high levels of cosmic rays in deep space will have the same effect as other kinds of ionizing radiation.

It can kill or damage cells in our bodies. And it can damage our DNA, too, which makes it much more likely that we'll get cancer.

And if there's a really bad radiation event, like a big burst of protons from the Sun? And you can't get into shelter on time?

That can just flat-out kill you.

But it *is* possible to protect yourself from this stuff, yeah?

Sure.

The old-fashioned way is to just surround yourself with a lot of mass—make your spacecraft's walls thicker and denser.

Or you could keep your water in tanks all around your living spaces.

Water's the best radiation shield that we know of, actually.

Folks would *love* to come up with a material that shields as well as water without weighing so much, but we're...not actually sure if that's possible?

Well, gee, is *that* all? Dissolving bones and galactic death rays?

Physically, anyway.

Mental health is a whole other thing.

We're talking about highly trained astronaut professionals.

Sure.

But even just living on the space station is hard, and most people are only there for a few months. Imagine what it'll be like to deal with those conditions for *years*.

Space vehicles are cramped. The fans that keep the air circulating are loud, and they're on *constantly*.

It might be hard to sleep, and that little cubby is your only private space.

If microgravity doesn't agree with you, you're low-level nauseated all the time. You can't do normal things that might relax you at home, like take a shower or cook.

Plus you're just living right up in the business of a bunch of other people, *all* the time.

Like, think of how antsy you get when there's a storm and you're stuck inside for a couple of days, and multiply that about a hundred times over.

Still, it can't be *that* much worse than the space station, right? And folks obviously figure out how to cope up there.

?

Sure. But keep in mind what the number one space station stress reliever is.

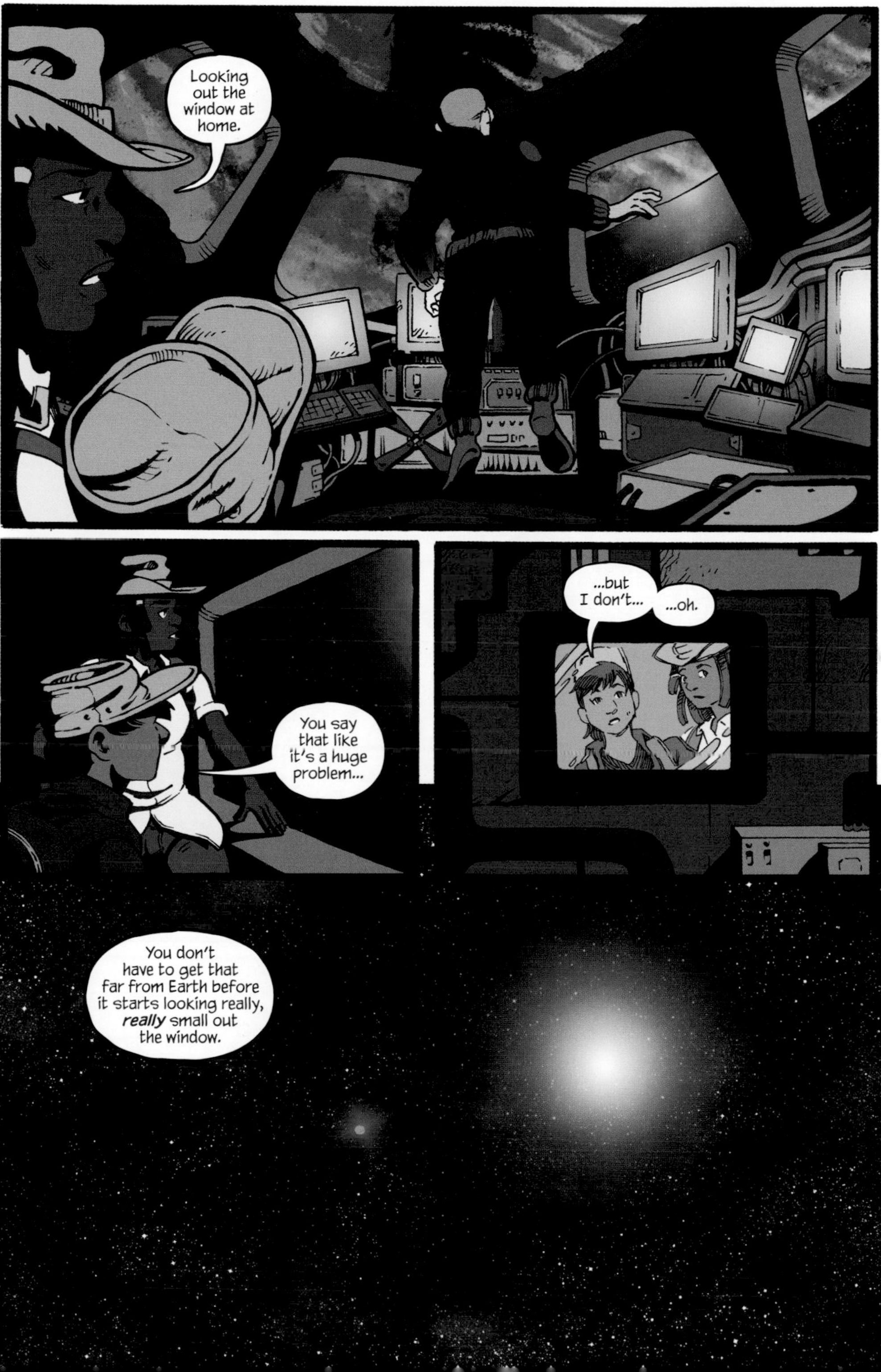
Looking out the window at home.
You say that like it's a huge problem...
...but I don't...
...oh.
You don't have to get that far from Earth before it starts looking really, *really* small out the window.

We have no idea what the psychological strain of being so far away from Earth will be.

We don't know what it'll do to a person to see nothing outside but stars or bare Martian rock for years and years.

You can be pretty isolated on Earth. Like, there're a bunch of permanent research stations on Antarctica.

True. And studying the people who live and work in places like that gives us some idea of what to expect.

We've even run a few analog studies—simulations of what a Mars mission would be like.

But honestly, there's no way to actually know what a real deep-space trip is going to do to people.

No human being has *ever* been as isolated as a Mars crew would be.

You can't simulate that kind of vulnerability.

But we can do it.

?

A human crew can handle going to Mars.

I think so, yeah.

Good.

Of course, actually *landing* on the planet is a whole other train wreck waiting to happen.

CHAPTER SIX: A LANDING YOU CAN WALK AWAY FROM

Right, you're just messing with me now.

What? No, no! Of course not!

Because landing is one thing we have *got* to know how to do at this point.

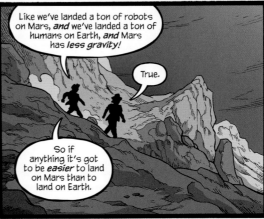

Like we've landed a ton of robots on Mars, *and* we've landed a ton of humans on Earth, *and* Mars has *less gravity!*

True.

So if anything it's got to be *easier* to land on Mars than to land on Earth.

...

Ellie.

I have nothing but confidence in the aerospace community's ability to crack the nut of human-scale Mars EDL, but we are a long way off from that day.

Pretty sure I caught an acronym in there.

EDL's shorthand for the whole "get yourself on the surface of Mars" process— Entry, Descent, and Landing.

You enter the Martian atmosphere, you descend toward the ground, and then you hopefully land in one piece.

And I hate to keep being a downer, but...

Ellie, *Come on.*

Look, it's really hard!

This may actually be the hardest-to-solve engineering problem out of everything we're gonna talk about today!

What? *How?*

Here's the thing about Mars: it has one-third of Earth's gravity, which is more than enough to cause problems. If you drop a vehicle from Martian orbit, it's gonna hit the ground real hard unless you do something to slow it down.

Mars *also* has an atmosphere that's about one percent as thick as the air at sea level on Earth.

Sure, but what's that *mean*, exactly?

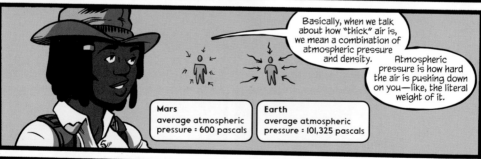

Basically, when we talk about how "thick" air is, we mean a combination of atmospheric pressure and density. Atmospheric pressure is how hard the air is pushing down on you—like, the literal weight of it.

Mars
average atmospheric pressure = 600 pascals

Earth
average atmospheric pressure = 101,325 pascals

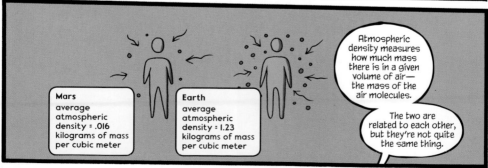

Atmospheric density measures how much mass there is in a given volume of air—the mass of the air molecules.

The two are related to each other, but they're not quite the same thing.

Mars
average atmospheric density = .016 kilograms of mass per cubic meter

Earth
average atmospheric density = 1.23 kilograms of mass per cubic meter

So the takeaway from all this is, "Mars has air but not a lot of it."

Yes. Enough atmosphere to burn your spacecraft up if you hit it too fast, or without enough protection.

But not enough to help you slow down nearly as much as the atmosphere on Earth would.

Didn't quite follow all that, but it sounds inconvenient.

Oh, yes.

So, backing up: the big issue to keep in mind when it comes to EDL is that it takes as much force to slow a thing down as it did to speed that thing up in the first place.

Burn engine to accelerate out of Earth orbit

Flip orientation

Burn engine to decelerate into Mars orbit

Newton's first law of motion, conservation of momentum.

Exactly.

So the delta-v that we need to get to Mars is the same as the delta-v we'll need to slow down enough to land there.

grin

I do actually listen to you.

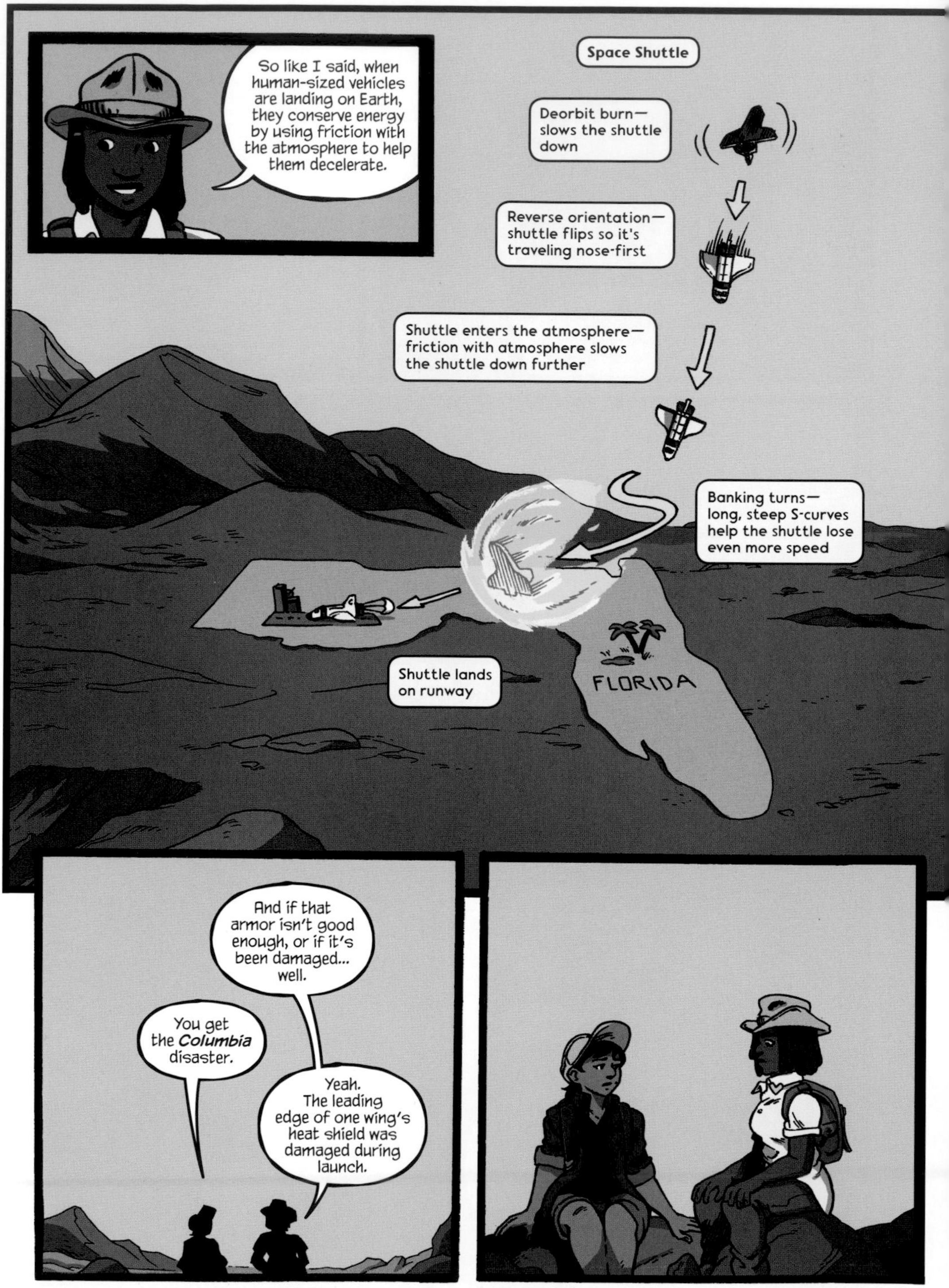

So like I said, when human-sized vehicles are landing on Earth, they conserve energy by using friction with the atmosphere to help them decelerate.
Space Shuttle
Deorbit burn— slows the shuttle down
Reverse orientation— shuttle flips so it's traveling nose-first
Shuttle enters the atmosphere— friction with atmosphere slows the shuttle down further
Banking turns— long, steep S-curves help the shuttle lose even more speed
Shuttle lands on runway
FLORIDA
And if that armor isn't good enough, or if it's been damaged... well.
You get the *Columbia* disaster.
Yeah. The leading edge of one wing's heat shield was damaged during launch.

Soyuz

Deorbit burn—slows the vehicle down

Orbital and service modules separate from descent module—the engines and the living quarters are discarded

Descent module enters the atmosphere—friction with atmosphere slows the descent module down further

That's why it's so important they're protected from heat. The shock wave of compressed air in front of the vehicle gets very, very hot, so you have to armor yourself against it.

Parachutes deploy—three stages of parachutes help the vehicle slow down further

KAZAKHSTAN

Soft landing engines fire—cushion the impact with the ground

Descent module lands

All right. That's how it works on Earth. Tell me how I'm gonna land on Mars.

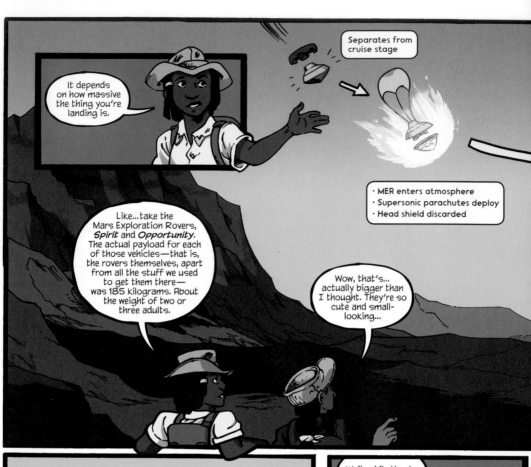

It depends on how massive the thing you're landing is.

Separates from cruise stage

· MER enters atmosphere
· Supersonic parachutes deploy
· Head shield discarded

Like...take the Mars Exploration Rovers, *Spirit* and *Opportunity*. The actual payload for each of those vehicles—that is, the rovers themselves, apart from all the stuff we used to get them there—was 185 kilograms. About the weight of two or three adults.

Wow, that's... actually bigger than I thought. They're so cute and small-looking...

They hit the atmosphere at about 19,000 kilometers an hour, and they slowed down using just the atmosphere—first with heat shields, then with supersonic parachutes.

Then the landers were lowered from their descent stages on very strong bridles—

Wait, while they're still falling? How's that work?

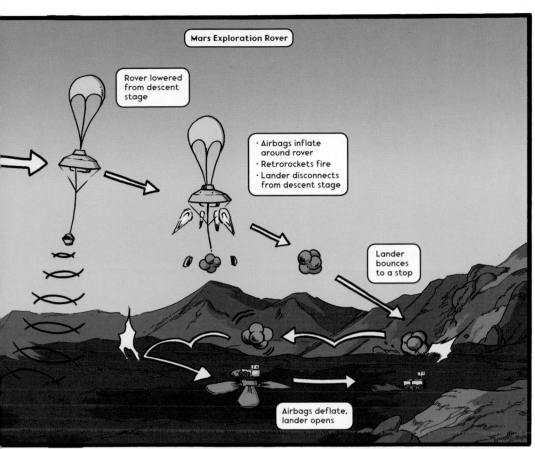

Mars Exploration Rover

Rover lowered from descent stage

- Airbags inflate around rover
- Retrorockets fire
- Lander disconnects from descent stage

Lander bounces to a stop

Airbags deflate, lander opens

With the parachute deployed, the whole descent stage was decelerating. So the momentum of the lander could carry it down the bridle bit by bit.

So it's falling from the thing that's falling.

Yes! Then they puffed up airbag cocoons, the descent stage fired retrorockets to slow down even more, then *snip!* Cut the rope.

Whoa, wait, we just... we bubble-wrapped *Spirit* and *Oppy* and cold *dropped* them onto Mars?

Yes, yes we did.

Okay, sure, I get why you wouldn't want to do that with people inside.

Not so much.

So how did we land *Curiosity*? It's the size of a car, that's gotta be closer to a people-friendly system.

Well, sure, *Curiosity*'s bigger than the Mars Exploration Rovers. The MSL *Curiosity*'s payload— like, the actual rover— was about 899 kilograms.

That's 300 kilograms more massive than anything else we've ever landed on Mars. *Way* too big for airbags to keep it safe while it bounced around.

Mars Exploration Rover— 2004–185 kilograms

MSL Curiosity— 2012–899 kilograms

Viking Landers— 1976–600 kilograms

Eleanor-shaped human— 75 kilograms

Plus, there's the matter of how big of a target you're hitting.

With *Spirit* and *Opportunity*, there was a lot of wiggle room.

Eagle Crater

Mars Exploration Rover Opportunity

Aiming for an ellipse 200 kilometers wide and 20 kilometers long

But with *Curiosity*, we wanted to look at specific things in a specific spot, surrounded by terrain that wasn't necessarily safe to land on...

So *Curiosity* was bigger *and* pickier.

Yeah.

How'd we do it?

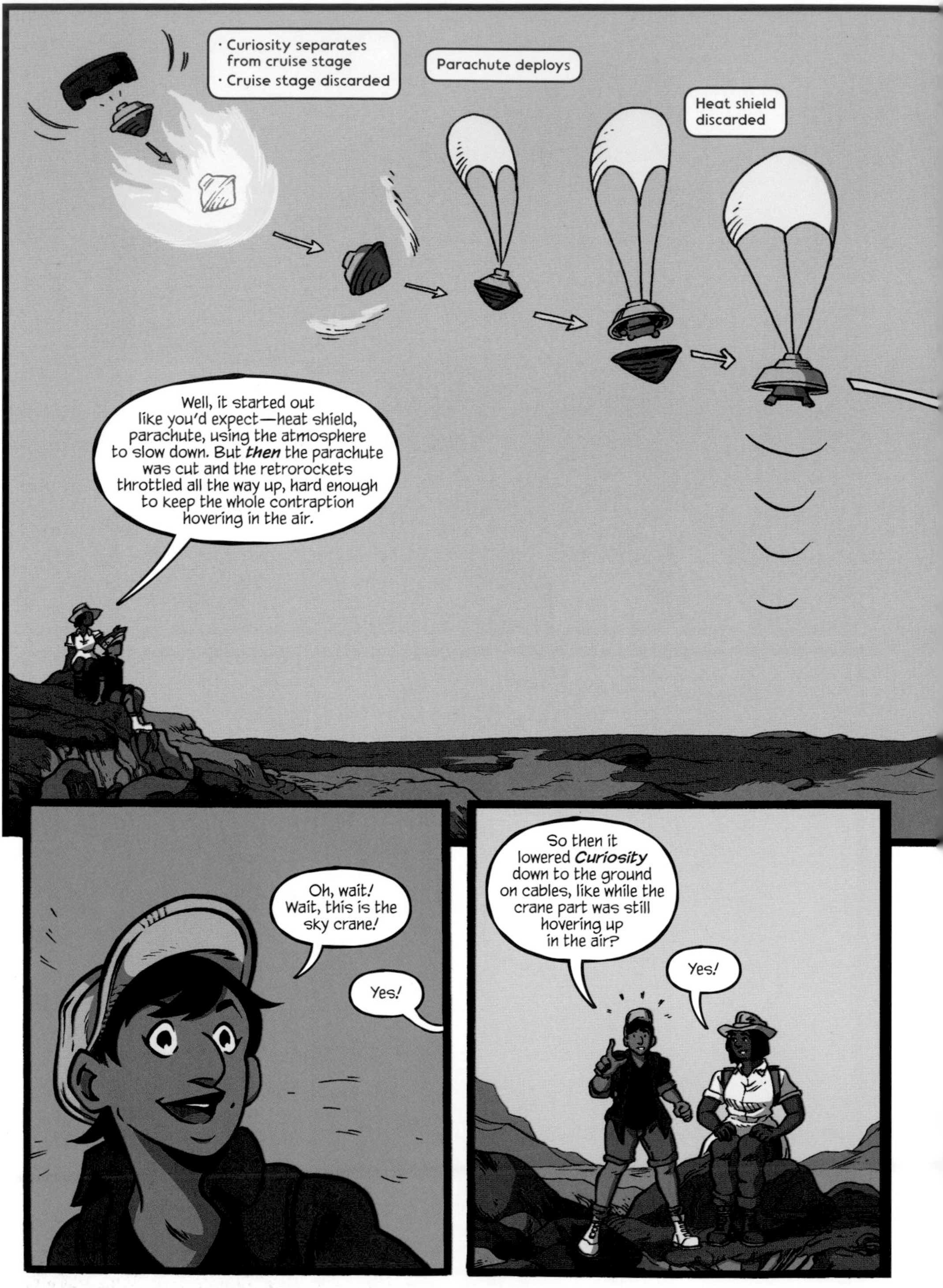
· Curiosity separates from cruise stage
· Cruise stage discarded
Parachute deploys
Heat shield discarded
Well, it started out like you'd expect—heat shield, parachute, using the atmosphere to slow down. But *then* the parachute was cut and the retrorockets throttled all the way up, hard enough to keep the whole contraption hovering in the air.
Oh, wait! Wait, this is the sky crane!
Yes!
So then it lowered *Curiosity* down to the ground on cables, like while the crane part was still hovering up in the air?
Yes!

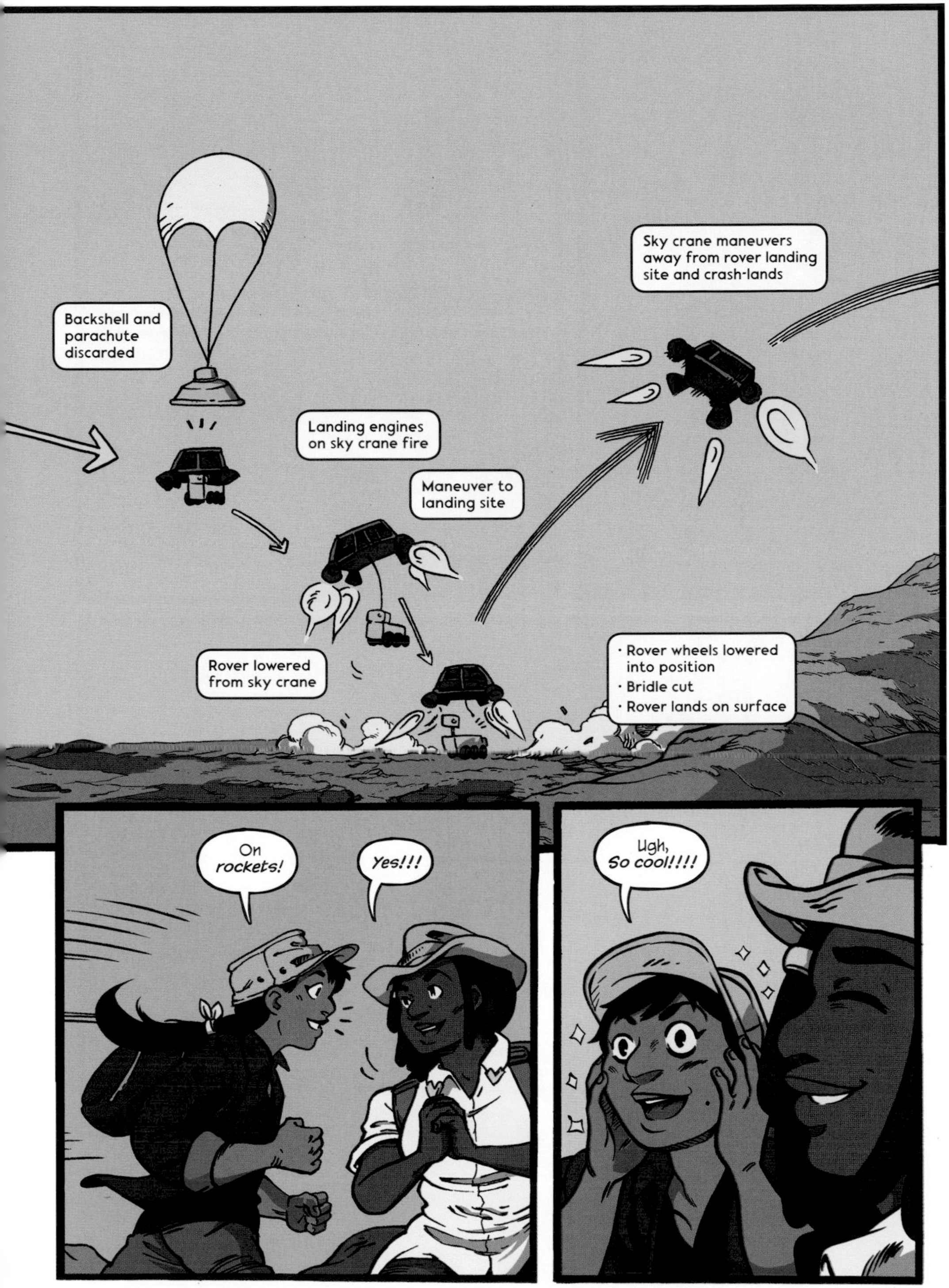
Backshell and parachute discarded
Landing engines on sky crane fire
Maneuver to landing site
Rover lowered from sky crane
Sky crane maneuvers away from rover landing site and crash-lands
· Rover wheels lowered into position
· Bridle cut
· Rover lands on surface
On *rockets!*
Yes!!!
Ugh, *So cool!!!!*

Man, why don't we just do that again? I'll ride a sky crane to Mars.

You... can't.

Why the heck not?

Because we've pushed this basic landing strategy about as far as it'll go.

Look, *Curiosity*'s big, but it's still only about the size of a car. A human-scale Mars lander would be more like a two-story house.

And if we're gonna land something as big as a house on Mars, our whole approach to the EDL problem has to change. Starting with how fast the vehicle is going when it first drops down into the atmosphere.

The problem is, you have to slow down a *lot* to settle into orbit around Mars, otherwise you'll either skip right off the atmosphere...

...or slam into the surface like a meteor, depending on how steep your angle of approach is. Neither of which are great options.

So can't we just spin the ship around and fire the engines?

You *could*, but it'd be nice if you didn't have to. Anything that involves "firing the engines" burns more fuel.

So it might make more sense to use aerobraking instead.

Use what now?

And more fuel means more mass.

Exactly.

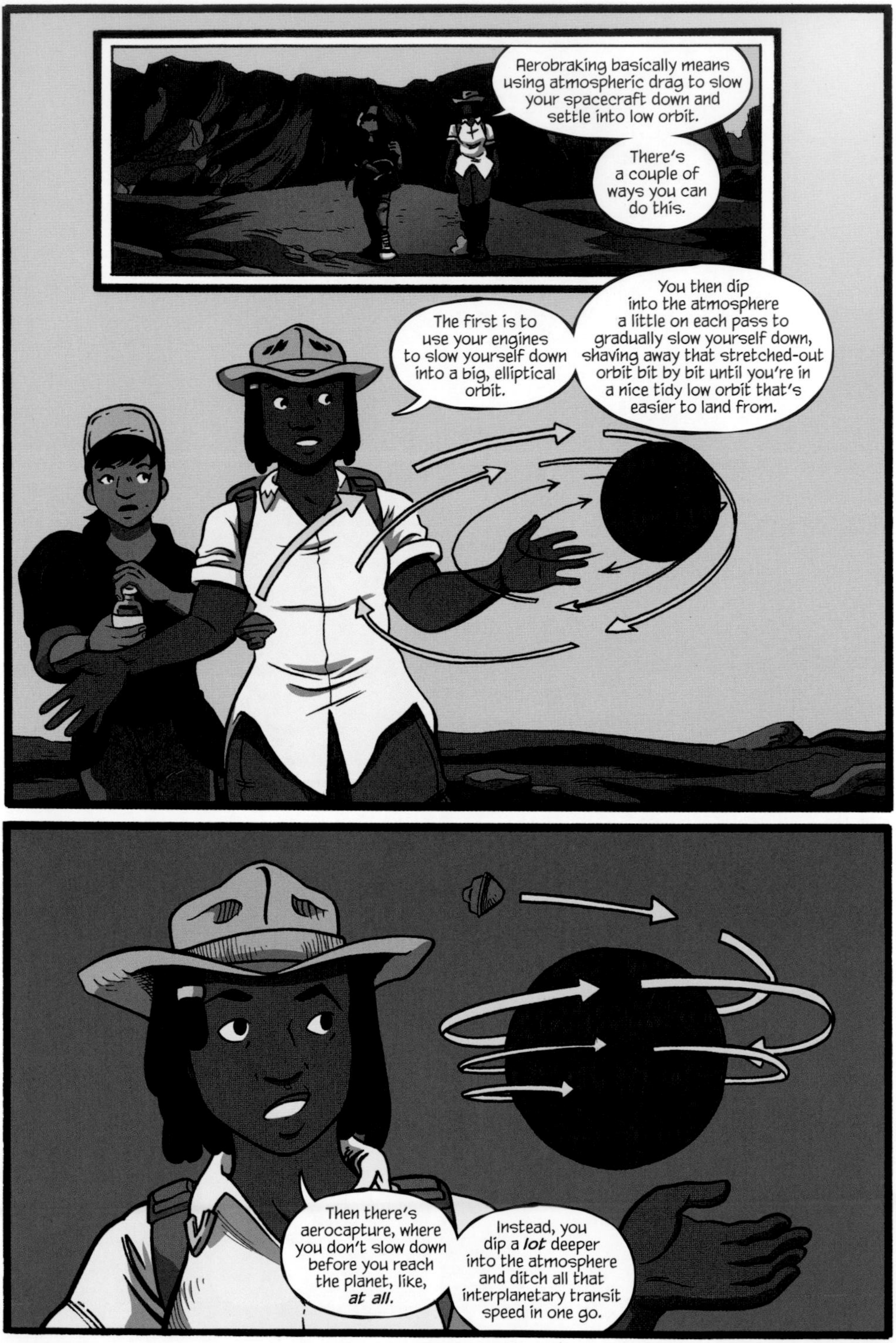
Aerobraking basically means using atmospheric drag to slow your spacecraft down and settle into low orbit.
There's a couple of ways you can do this.
The first is to use your engines to slow yourself down into a big, elliptical orbit.
You then dip into the atmosphere a little on each pass to gradually slow yourself down, shaving away that stretched-out orbit bit by bit until you're in a nice tidy low orbit that's easier to land from.
Then there's aerocapture, where you don't slow down before you reach the planet, like, *at all*.
Instead, you dip a *lot* deeper into the atmosphere and ditch all that interplanetary transit speed in one go.

How's that different from what *Curiosity* did? You're slowing down with a heat shield, right?

With *Curiosity*, we were aiming straight for the ground, without orbiting Mars first. So time was a huge issue—all we had was the air between open space and the surface to work with.

From Earth-Mars transit to Martian orbit

From Earth-Mars transit to the Martian surface

We can't use *Curiosity*'s EDL for a crew because there just isn't enough time—enough air—to slow down that way.

But with aerocapture, you're not aiming for the ground, you're aiming for orbit. Once you dip into the atmosphere, you're dragging through it for a very long distance before you loop back out again.

And *then* we can just do what *Curiosity* did, right? Parachutes, sky crane—

We are almost definitely not going to be using a parachute.

What? Why *not*?

Too big of a lander, going too fast. The atmosphere isn't even thick enough for parachutes until you're like twenty kilometers above the Martian surface. The math just doesn't work—you can't slow a human-scale lander down that much in twenty kilometers' worth of Martian air.

So make a bigger parachute!

It'd have to be the size of a football stadium. It's not gonna happen.

But! How about rockets?

Always on board for rockets.

So, retropropulsion is when you fire your engine in the direction you're traveling in and slow yourself down.

Yeah, we've been over this. And since we know how to build rockets already, we're set, right?

Well. Remember, at this point you've slowed down a lot, but you'll still hit the atmosphere at supersonic speeds. And these rockets will scream toward the ground nozzle-first. And Martian air is thin, but when you're moving through it faster than sound, that's still *windy as heck.*

We're just not sure how a rocket engine's gonna react to those conditions. Or even what *type* of engine we should use.

We can run computer simulations, sure, but actually building prototypes and testing them meaningfully is gonna be hard.

Hmm. That's all very interesting, Eleanor.

But I think the real question is...

Will there be a sky crane?

Maybe?

!!!!!

That's one way of dealing with the last big problem...

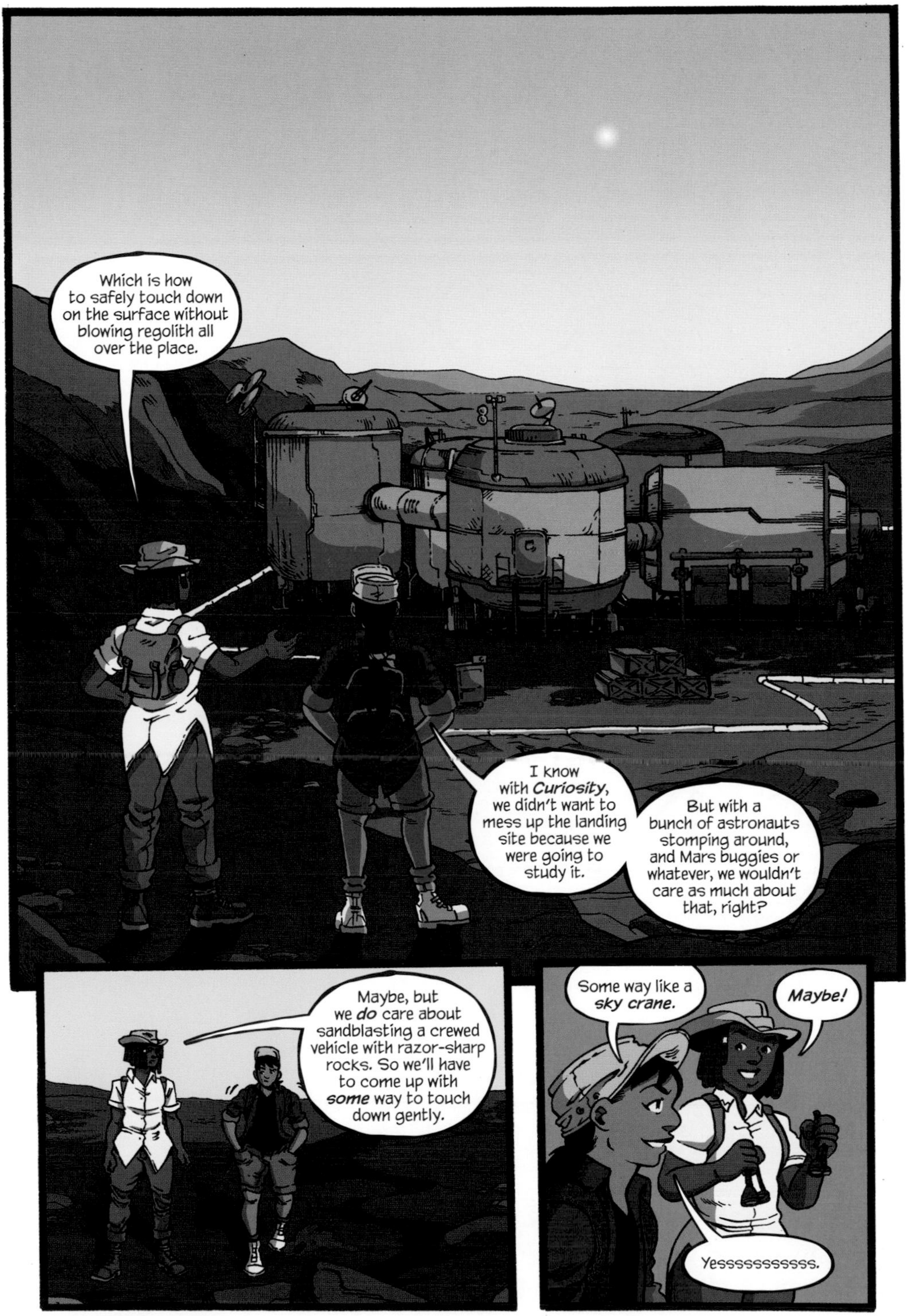
Which is how to safely touch down on the surface without blowing regolith all over the place.
I know with *Curiosity*, we didn't want to mess up the landing site because we were going to study it.
But with a bunch of astronauts stomping around, and Mars buggies or whatever, we wouldn't care as much about that, right?
Maybe, but we *do* care about sandblasting a crewed vehicle with razor-sharp rocks. So we'll have to come up with *some* way to touch down gently.
Some way like a *sky crane.*
Maybe!
Yesssssssssss.

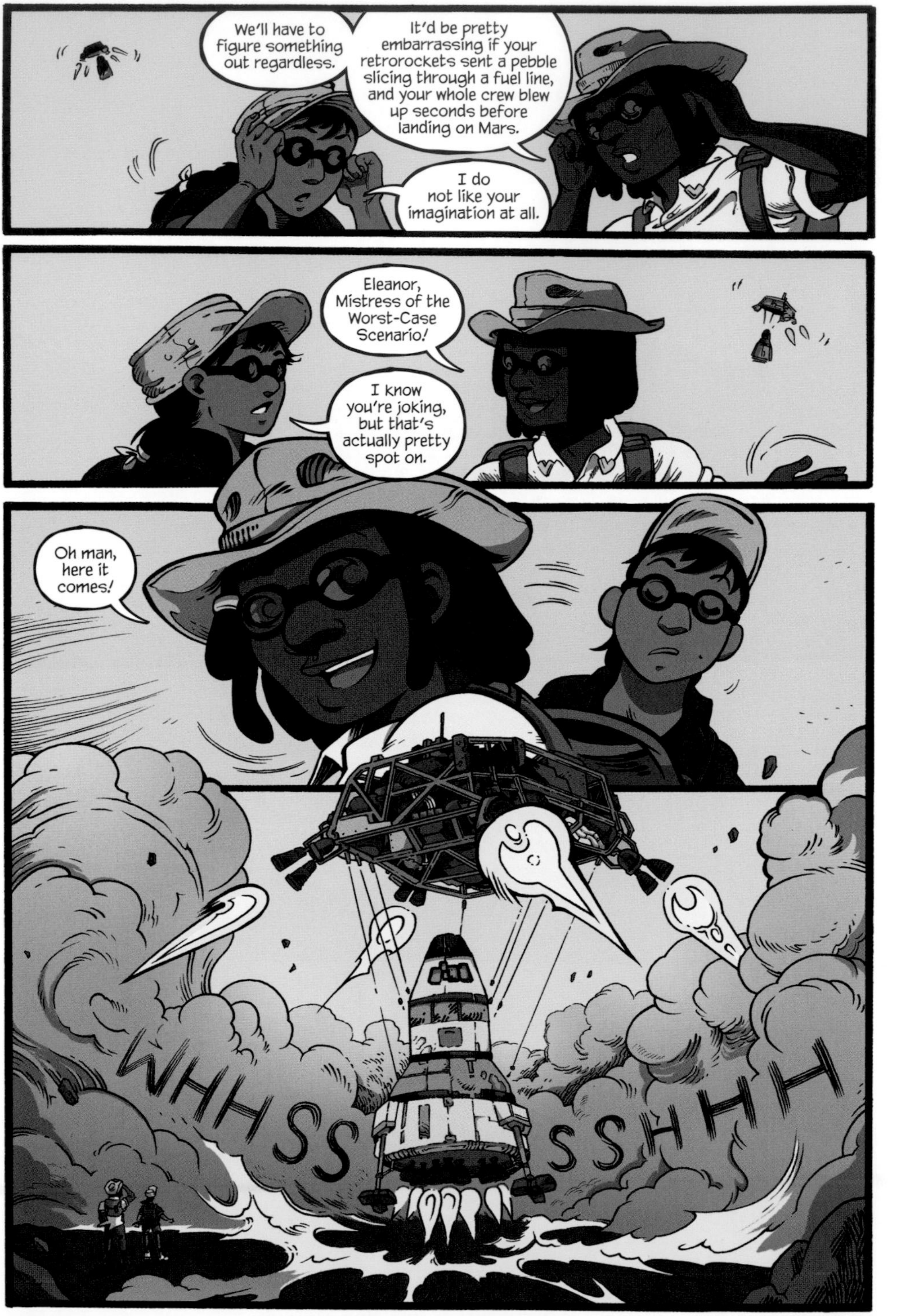
We'll have to figure something out regardless.
It'd be pretty embarrassing if your retrorockets sent a pebble slicing through a fuel line, and your whole crew blew up seconds before landing on Mars.
I do not like your imagination at all.
Eleanor, Mistress of the Worst-Case Scenario!
I know you're joking, but that's actually pretty spot on.
Oh man, here it comes!
WHHSS SSHHH

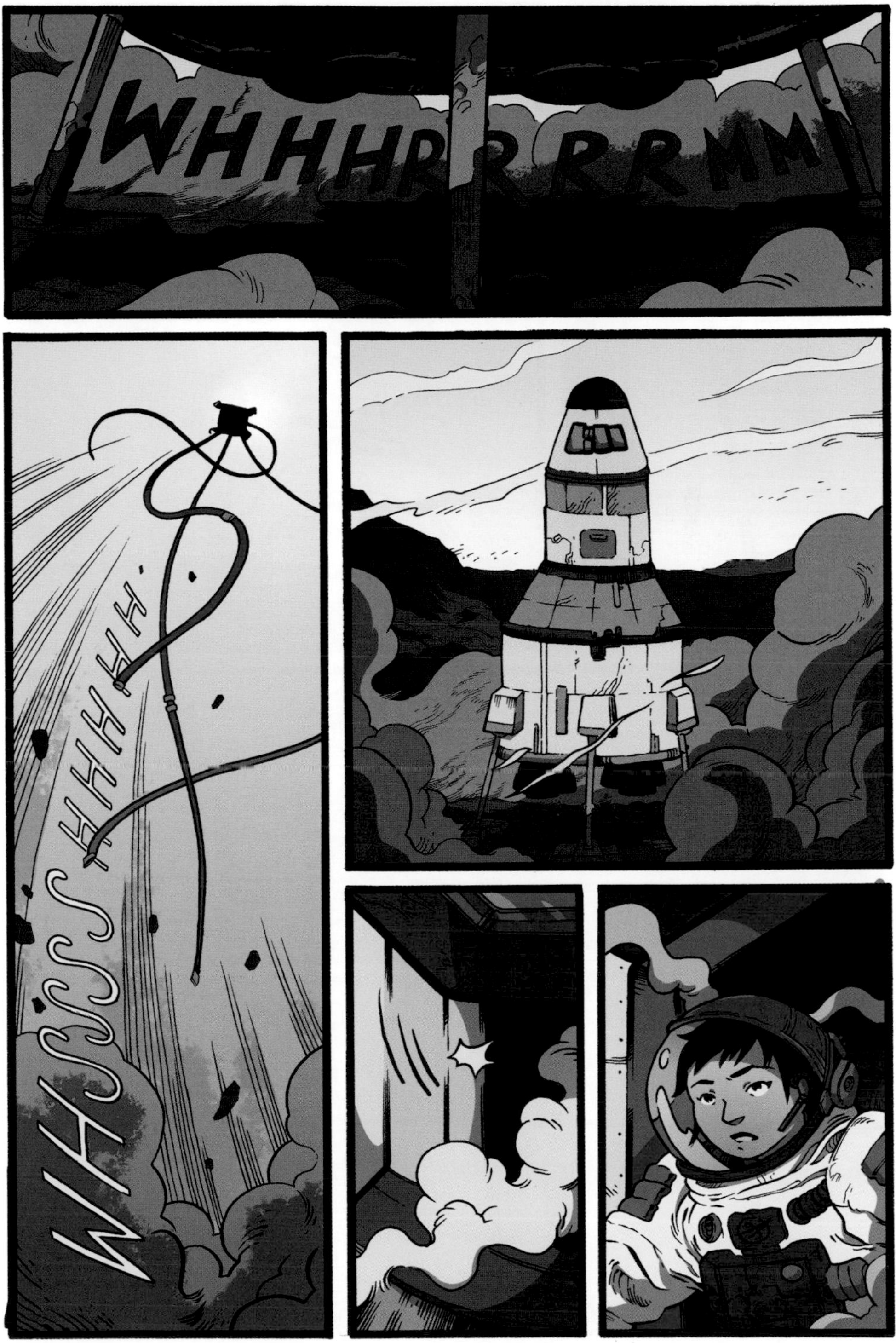
WHHHRRRRMM
WHSSHHHHHH

Of course, even once we land safe and sound, we still have to *stay* safe and sound for months and months and months on a planet where we can't breathe or eat or drink anything we haven't brought along or made ourselves.

Ellie, oh my god.

CHAPTER SEVEN: DON'T DIE ON MARS

You keep telling me about how Mars is like a barren airless wasteland, so why is living on Mars any different than living in space?

You still have to be in a sealed-up habitat or a suit all the time.

Habitat must-haves:
· Carbon dioxide removal
· Trace contaminant control
· Oxygen generator
· Water recovery
· Temperature and humidity control
· Air circulation
· Fire detection and suppression
· Toilet
· Shower

There's gravity on Mars, for one thing.

It's about 38% of the strength of Earth's gravity, but that's a heck of a lot better than nothing.

Healthier for the crew, right?

Yes!

Gravity also means that we won't have to work as hard to keep air circulating through the habitat and that liquid will move more like the way we're used to...

...and that the crew won't have to put Velcro on everything to keep it from floating away.

Plus, we'll be able to drink our hard-earned *"Holy geez, we woke up on Mars"* cups of coffee out of real mugs instead of plastic bags.

The strain of spending months and months in that tiny transit vehicle is gonna be intense.

Living on a planet again, with more space to move around and more *stuff* to do, will be a massive mental-health boost to the crew. Not to mention having an actual landscape to look at outside the windows.

Forget looking at it! We'll be running all over the place the minute we get our gravity legs back.

Well, sure. That's the point of sending a human crew all the way there, right? To get out and see the planet for themselves and make discoveries far beyond what a robot would really be capable of.

Yes! Exactly!

All we have to do is figure out how to make a Mars surface suit that can protect humans from radiation, has joints that won't lock up with dust, and is lightweight enough for someone to walk around in.

Wait, wait, wait. Hold on.

Holding.

Radiation? But this is on the surface of a planet.

What about the Martian magnetosphere?

Funny thing, there isn't one.

Well, why the heck not?!

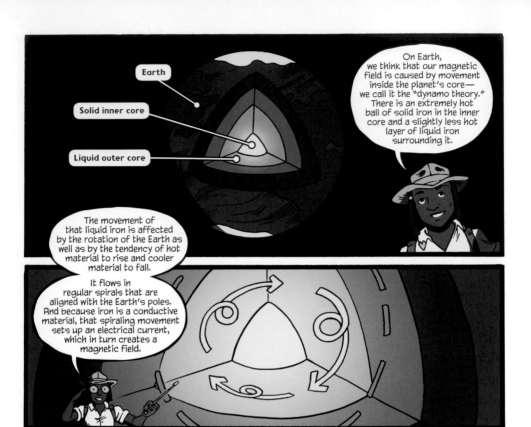

Earth

Solid inner core

Liquid outer core

On Earth, we think that our magnetic field is caused by movement inside the planet's core—we call it the "dynamo theory." There is an extremely hot ball of solid iron in the inner core and a slightly less hot layer of liquid iron surrounding it.

The movement of that liquid iron is affected by the rotation of the Earth as well as by the tendency of hot material to rise and cooler material to fall.

It flows in regular spirals that are aligned with the Earth's poles. And because iron is a conductive material, that spiraling movement sets up an electrical current, which in turn creates a magnetic field.

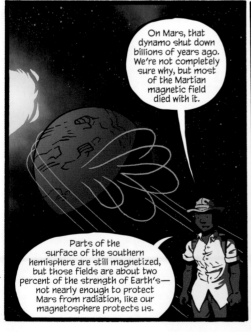

On Mars, that dynamo shut down billions of years ago. We're not completely sure why, but most of the Martian magnetic field died with it.

Parts of the surface of the southern hemisphere are still magnetized, but those fields are about two percent of the strength of Earth's—not nearly enough to protect Mars from radiation, like our magnetosphere protects us.

So if we can't figure out a lightweight material that adequately shields against radiation, we'll have to pretty seriously limit how much time the crew spends outside under an open sky.

144

Okay, radiation's a problem. Fine. Dust?

Fine is exactly right.

?

The dust in your house is mostly made up of organic things, like dead skin cells, pollen, fiber from our clothes, bits of paper, dandruff, insects, all kinds of stuff.

And on Earth, moisture on the ground or in the atmosphere causes dust to clump together.

On Mars, where water in the soil is almost always frozen and the air is not only dry but thin, this doesn't happen.

All the bits of dust that have been banging around the surface for millions of years, grinding up against each other and getting smaller and smaller? It's in such teeny tiny particles that we don't even call it dust, really—we call it "fines."

It gets into *everything*. And it's very, very sharp.

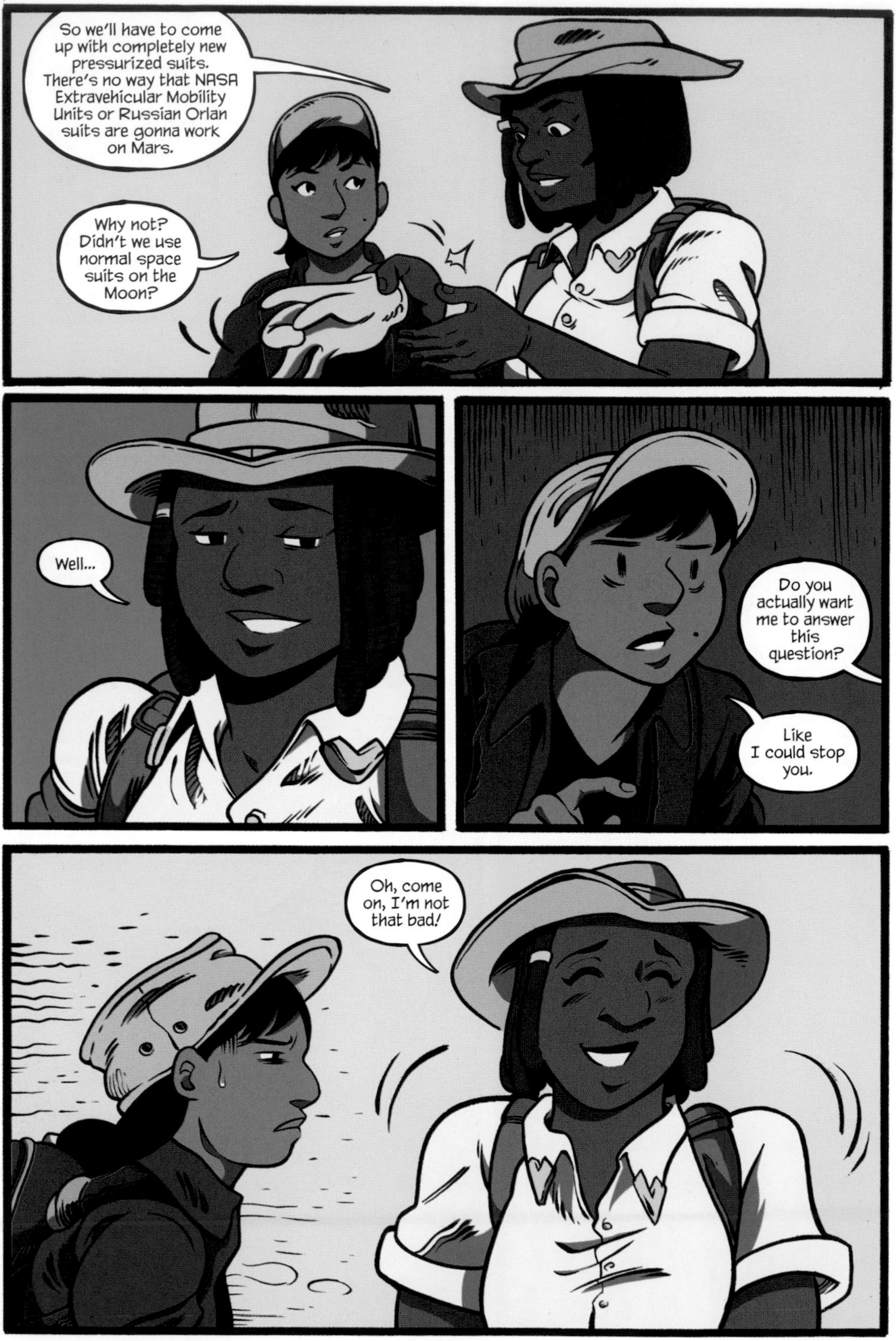
So we'll have to come up with completely new pressurized suits. There's no way that NASA Extravehicular Mobility Units or Russian Orlan suits are gonna work on Mars.
Why not? Didn't we use normal space suits on the Moon?
Well...
Do you actually want me to answer this question?
Like I could stop you.
Oh, come on, I'm not that bad!

The Apollo astronauts wore one-piece suits of mostly soft material, with metal rings where the helmets and gloves attached.

Just like modern space suits, they were made up of layers.

The outer layer was an "Integrated Thermal Micrometeoroid Garment" that protected astronauts from the Sun, abrasion with the lunar fines, and micrometeoroid impacts.

On parts of the suit that would get roughed up, like the gloves and the boots and the knees, there were patches of woven steel and Teflon-coated cloth.

Sounds reasonable.

But when NASA studied the suits after they'd been used on the Moon, it turned out they'd gotten real beat up, *real* quickly.

The outer fabric was worn through in places, and sharp lunar particles had worked down into the fragile under-layers of the suit, along with tiny bits of broken-up Teflon fibers. Which are made of *glass*, by the way.

Yikes.

The Apollo suits still had Moon dust on them three decades later. Imagine how dusty they must have been when the astronauts first took them off.

And dust is bad news, right?

Right. If it can tear up a space suit like that, imagine what it'd do to your skin. Or your eyes. Or your *lungs*.

Hmm.

Anyway, those are the only suits we've ever made that were designed to be used on another planet, and they...

Kinda sucked.

A little, yeah.

I still don't get why we can't just make some changes to the space suits we're using now. They work fine!

Sure, in microgravity.

But the NASA EMUs...

Eleanor.

The NASA Extravehicular Mobility Units, also called space suits, weigh like 145 kilograms.

Sure, Mars gravity isn't as strong, but that's a *lot* of extra weight to be dragging around with you while you're trying to do your job.

New suits it is, then.

Okay, so, in the "positive" column we have gravity and scenery, and in the "negative" column we have killer dust...and also gravity?

Living on planets is messy!

But that's why we're going to Mars, right? To study all that good, good mess.

POP

And, hey, physical planet stuff can also be dead useful for staying alive.

If we're feeling frugal and a little bit ambitious, we can wring some consumables right out of the ground. And the air, too. Honestly, that would be easier.

I know you don't mean literally wring them out like a wet towel, but I'm drawing a blank here.

There's more water on Mars than we used to think, but most of it's frozen—either in big ice caps at the poles, or under the regolith.

So in order to get access to that water, we have to process a ton of regolith and squeeze all the moisture out of it.

That kind of process is called ISRU—In-Situ Resource Utilization.

ISRU Plant—Regolith

Excavator

Water extraction happens in here somewhere

Waste

Gonna have to unpack that one a little bit more.

"In situ" is Latin, and it translates to "on site" or "in position."

Oh, so it's about using the resources that're already on the planet.

Exactly.

Regolith processing would be a great way to get water, which is *super handy.*

But we have no idea if it'll ever be practical, or even possible. When you're digging chunks out of the ground and trying to move them through a machine, there's just a lot that can go wrong.

Like a pebble getting stuck in a gear.

Yeah, exactly. And we haven't solved those problems yet.

Plus, this thing would have to chew through *a lot* of Mars, which would tear up the surface of the planet pretty badly. And not everyone's okay with that.

Understandable.

But regolith mining isn't the only kind of ISRU!

A lot of folks think we should concentrate on mining the Martian air instead. It's *really* thin, and it's almost 96% carbon dioxide, but we can turn that CO2 into oxygen. Which the crew can then use *not only* to breathe but as the oxidizer for the rocket that'll get them back into Martian orbit again.

We're actually sending a little experimental ISRU plant on the 2020 Mars rover. It's called *MOXIE.*

Cute.

Mars 2020 Rover

Set to arrive on Mars in February 2021

Stands for "Mars Oxygen ISRU Experiment."

Less cute.

It'll collect carbon dioxide from the atmosphere, compress it so that it's at about the same pressure as air on Earth.

Mars Oxygen ISRU Experiment

Then split it into oxygen and carbon, and then test the oxygen for purity.

That new rover will improve on a bunch of *Curiosity's* systems. Better EDL, optical zoom on the mast camera, a microscopic camera inside its spectrometer to look for signs of microbes in the dust, subsurface radar imaging. Cool stuff!

Nice.

POP!!

Anyway! Moving on.

No worries.

Nadia, she's gonna be so great.

Always up for rovers.

So all of this seems pretty cool, but...

Won't it take a while? You keep saying how thin Martian air is...

I do, and you're right. An atmospheric processing plant like this would have to run a long time to collect much oxygen.

Is this the kind of thing you meant with that whole "send our luggage first" thing?

Yeah, exactly! It'd be great to launch all this support equipment ahead of time.

Like the surface habitat, power plant, ISRU equipment, the containers we'll store the consumables in...

...whatever rovers or buggies or whatever we plan to use...

Tell me about Mars cars.

Well...we'll probably need at least one!

Really? You're not just messing with me?

Yeah, unless we want the crew to be stuck looking at the inevitably boring flat rock plain we choose for a landing site.

Okay, quick side question, *why* would we go all the way to Mars just to land on something boring?

Because boring is safer, mostly.

Like, that's why getting *Curiosity's* EDL just right was such a huge deal.

If we'd screwed that up, we might have dropped the rover onto a mountainside...

...and had the whole thing flip over.

We're *reeallly* gonna want to avoid that kind of thing when we're landing a crew. So we'll pick a nice, smooth, level landing site.

We'll use robotic rovers to check things out that're either too far away or too dangerous for people to look at directly.

And we'll give the crew one or more surface vehicles to drive around in.

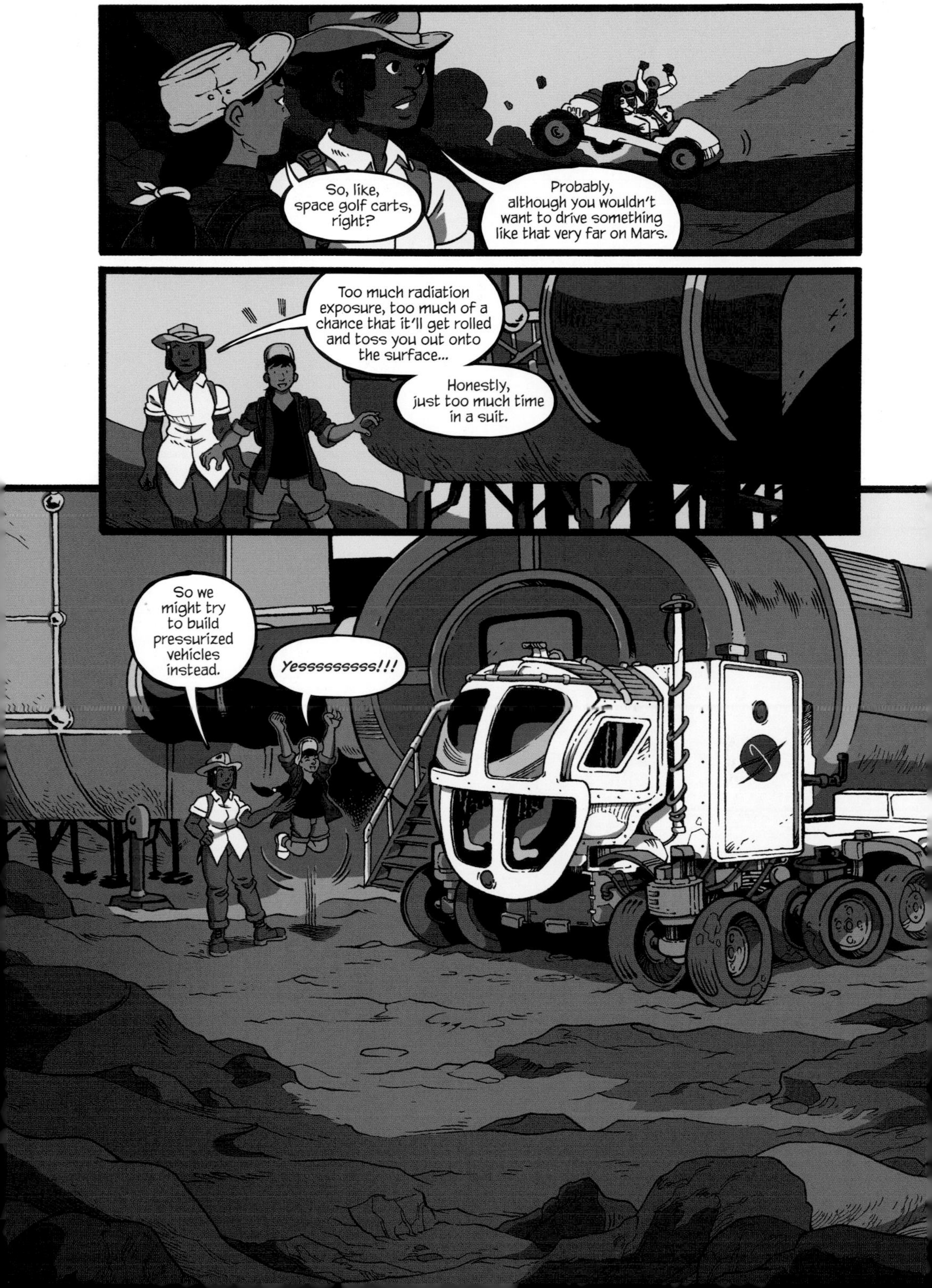
So, like, space golf carts, right?
Probably, although you wouldn't want to drive something like that very far on Mars.
Too much radiation exposure, too much of a chance that it'll get rolled and toss you out onto the surface...
Honestly, just too much time in a suit.
So we might try to build pressurized vehicles instead.
Yessssssssss!!!

Functionally, it would be a little shirtsleeve compartment you could carry around with you while you explore the planet.

Shirt...?

Oh, sorry, that just means a compartment where you don't have to wear a pressure suit.

Got it. So like a little laboratory on wheels, right?

And a backup habitat.

Look, if your life-support system breaks down on Mars, you want to be able to go somewhere else to breathe while you fix it.

Like what if it takes a week? You gonna stay in your surface suit that whole time?

Hard pass on that one.

Diaper rash would be killer.

Gross.

Sorry.

So, how are we powering all of this stuff?

Prooooooobably a little nuclear plant on the surface?

Brings up some safety issues, but it would be a lot less finicky to deal with than solar panels.

It could power the hab and any ISRU plants, plus recharge electric vehicles.

Curiosity's nuclear, right?

Yep, and that's one reason it's more robust than the Mars Exploration Rovers.

Both of the Mars Exploration Rovers used solar power, which helped keep them more lightweight, but most of their operation difficulties had to do with not enough sunlight hitting their solar cells.

That's why we lost communication with the *Spirit* MER rover. It actually survived a few winters by parking on sunny slopes, but one year it got stuck on flat ground with too much dust on its solar panels.

You're saying that *Spirit* froze to death?

That is a grim but accurate way to put it.

Poor kid.

Look, if your hab uses solar panels for power on Mars, you can go outside and clean them off if they get too dusty.

But you'll also have way better things to do.

So we're gonna go nuclear?

Looking likely!

Nice.

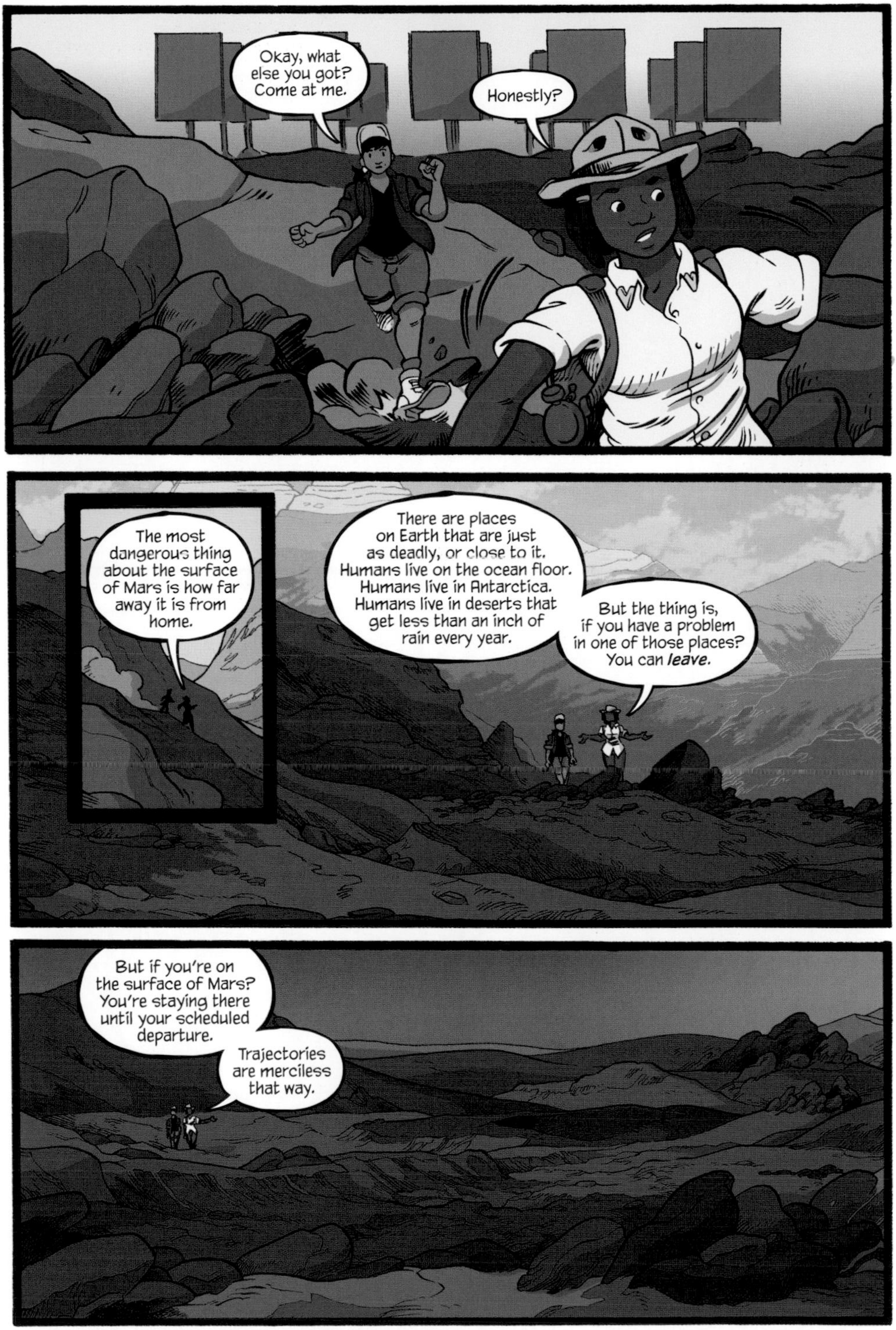
Okay, what else you got? Come at me.
Honestly?
The most dangerous thing about the surface of Mars is how far away it is from home.
There are places on Earth that are just as deadly, or close to it. Humans live on the ocean floor. Humans live in Antarctica. Humans live in deserts that get less than an inch of rain every year.
But the thing is, if you have a problem in one of those places? You can *leave*.
But if you're on the surface of Mars? You're staying there until your scheduled departure.
Trajectories are merciless that way.

If you have an emergency, the only thing that Earth can give you is time-delayed advice.

If you break your arm, or if a meteorite blasts a hole in your habitat, or if your rover breaks down while you're out doing a survey?

The only people who can physically help you with your physical problem are the other members of your crew, using only the tools and equipment you brought with you.

So you're forced to be a survivalist basically.

I mean, yeah, in a way! It really just hammers home...

You know, we've spent so much time talking about engineering and technology challenges...

...but in a lot of ways the most important piece of a successful crewed Mars mission will be the crew themselves.

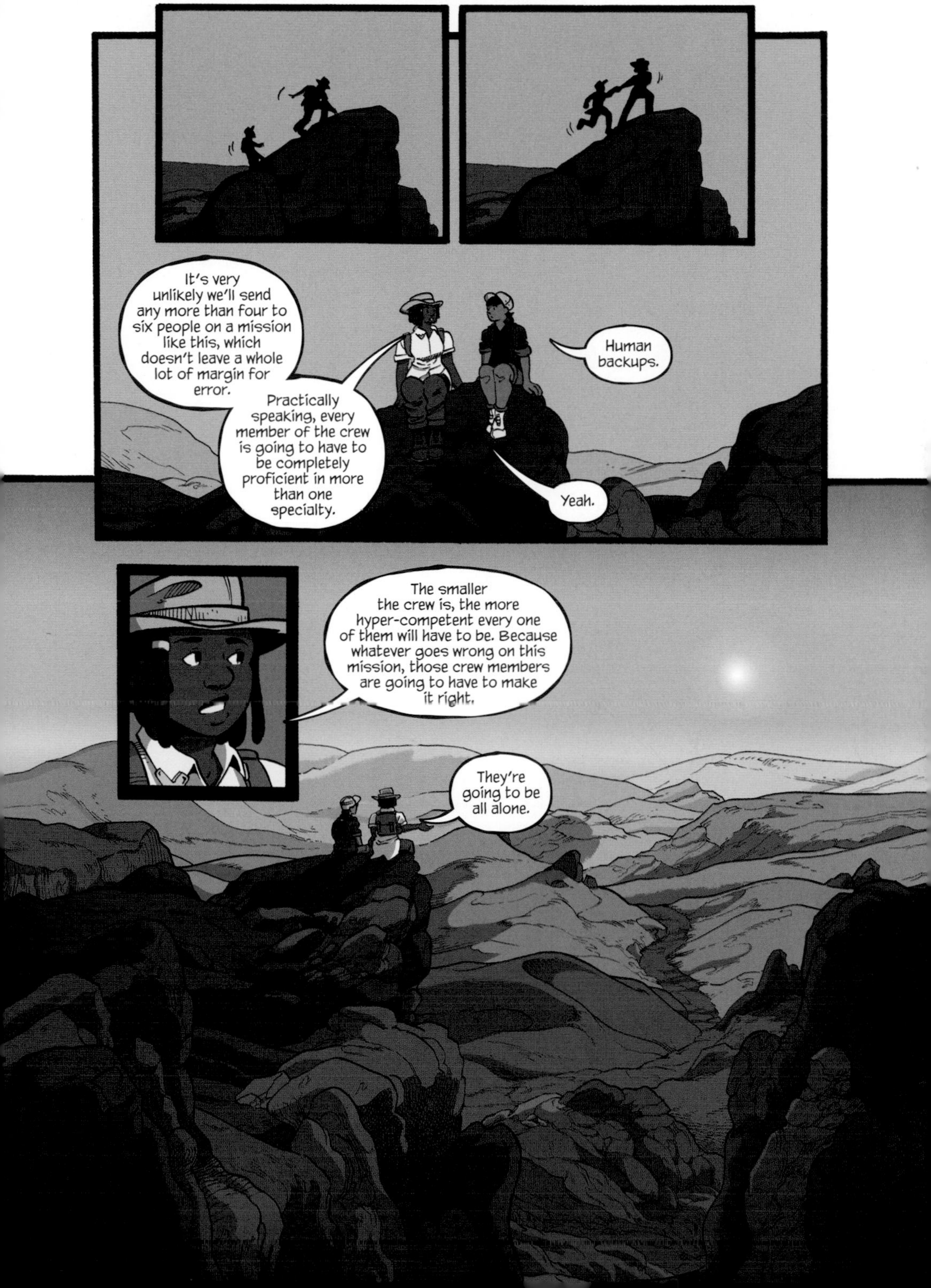

It's very unlikely we'll send any more than four to six people on a mission like this, which doesn't leave a whole lot of margin for error.
Human backups.
Practically speaking, every member of the crew is going to have to be completely proficient in more than one specialty.
Yeah.
The smaller the crew is, the more hyper-competent every one of them will have to be. Because whatever goes wrong on this mission, those crew members are going to have to make it right.
They're going to be all alone.

CHAPTER EIGHT:
GETTING HOME AGAIN

Okay. So let's say we've gotten up and out of Earth's gravity well, we've crossed millions of kilometers of deep space, we've landed on another planet, we've done all the cool science and taken all the amazing Mars selfies, and we haven't died.

Now the hard part's over, right? We've solved all the big problems, all that's left is going home.

Sort of.

What do you mean "sort of"?

Well, yeah, the last thing you'd have to do is get back to Earth, but that's not exactly a little problem.

You're not serious.

Look, I've been paying attention! The transit vehicle that we used to get to Mars would still be in orbit, right? Along with all the food and air and water that we need for the trip back to Earth. And we would've sent the go-home rocket ahead of time with all the other luggage.

Probably!

So all that needs to get launched back up into orbit is, like, whatever Mars rocks we want to bring home with us, the crew, and enough air so that we don't suffocate on the way up.

Plus, like, snacks.

Snacks are good.

And we spent allllllll that time talking about the rocket equation, so I *know* that this rocket won't even have to be that big!

We won't be carrying nearly as much stuff, *and* Mars has less gravity, so that whole "burning fuel to launch the fuel you haven't burned yet" exponential cycle thing won't be nearly as bad, right?

That is absolutely true.

So what's the problem?

Infrastructure.

Well.

?

Lack of infrastructure.

What, you mean like... a launch pad?

That's part of it.

So we'll just build one.

Can we back up a little?

There are three basic sets of things that you need in order to get yourself off a planetary surface and into orbit.

A launch vehicle, fuel for that vehicle, and a structure from which to launch that vehicle.

So a rocket to get us back up off of Mars, rocket fuel, and a launch pad.

We know how to build rockets, and you're right, we can totally send a Martian launch vehicle ahead with the other cargo.

But there are a lot of unknowns here.

Are we going to have to send it in pieces?

If it's in pieces, does it put itself together automatically?

Will the ground team use robots to assemble it remotely from Earth?

Will the crew have to do it themselves after they arrive?

If we're sending a fully assembled rocket to Mars, how do we land something like that? Can we hit a target as small as a launch platform, or will we have to move it over to that platform later?

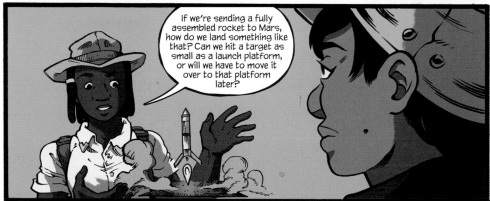

But let's assume we've figured out how to get our launch vehicle to Mars.

What about fueling it?

If we use cryo propellants, where is that fuel coming from? Are we making it with ISRU? *Can* we make it with ISRU? Are we sending it from Earth in tanks?

What kind of storage system will we need to keep it cold enough for what's probably gonna be multiple years?

How will we get the fuel *into* the rocket when it's time for the crew to come home?

And all of this is assuming we'll even use liquid propellants, which we might not!

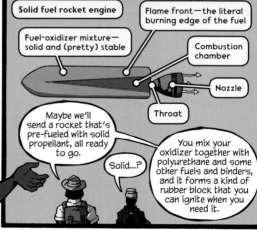

Solid fuel rocket engine

Fuel-oxidizer mixture—solid and (pretty) stable

Flame front—the literal burning edge of the fuel

Combustion chamber

Nozzle

Throat

Maybe we'll send a rocket that's pre-fueled with solid propellant, all ready to go.

Solid...?

You mix your oxidizer together with polyurethane and some other fuels and binders, and it forms a kind of rubber block that you can ignite when you need it.

The risk of explosion is higher with solid propellants, though.

Not ideal.

They're also less efficient, but maybe that won't be a problem with a launch out of one-third g?

Just say "gravity." It's two extra syllables.

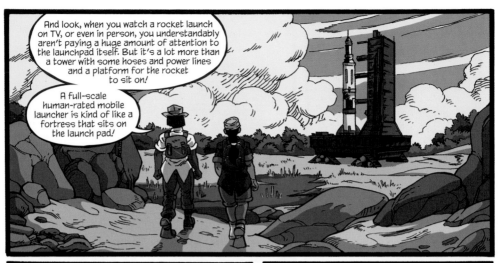

And look, when you watch a rocket launch on TV, or even in person, you understandably aren't paying a huge amount of attention to the launchpad itself. But it's a lot more than a tower with some hoses and power lines and a platform for the rocket to sit on!

A full-scale human-rated mobile launcher is kind of like a fortress that sits on the launch pad!

Mobile launcher

It has a pressurized interior where astronauts get ready to board the vehicle and where support staff can work. There's an umbilical tower with supply lines and an elevator for the crew. And separate from the platform you have storage tanks for cryo fuels and tanks for the water they flood the pad with during launch in order to dampen the shock waves of sound.

Why's it called a "mobile launcher"?

Because it *moves.*

The launcher starts out in a vehicle assembly building, where the rocket and the payload are stacked together.

Then *huge* vehicles called crawler-transporters *pick up* the *entire* thing and carry it to the launch pad.

That's... *wow.*

Isn't it?

So I guess there's, like...a control room somewhere?

There's a launch control center a safe distance away, yeah. Folks monitor and control the launch from the "firing room."

Good name.

And that's the other thing, there's a whole big team of *people* who watch the launch as it's happening, and can stop it very quickly if there's a problem.

Sometimes a launch is scrubbed with hardly any time left on the clock.

But they won't be able to do that on Mars, because of the comm delay.

Exactly.

I'm sure we'll automate the launch as much as we can, but there are things the crew're going to have to do for themselves. Which is pretty nerve-racking!

And they'll have a limited launch window, too, which they *cannot* miss if they want to get back to Earth again.

So I... guess we'll have to build a launchpad fortress thing? On Mars?

Maybe?

You *just* said—

I told you how crew launches work on *Earth*. But we've never done anything that's even in the same *category* as launching a rocket from Mars.

That's what you've said about, like, half of the stuff we've gone over today.

Well, this is even *more* of a totally new thing.

How is it a totally new thing?

Because every single time we've sent anything to Mars it's been a one-way trip.

Huh.

We've only just started serious plans for a sample return mission. This isn't a matter of improving or adapting existing systems to do a new and more difficult thing—this is almost starting from scratch.

It's in the "sky crane" category of spaceflight problems.

What?

Hang on, let me explain.

When we designed the *Curiosity* rover, we realized that it was going to be too big to land on Mars with the EDL technology we already had. But this wasn't a problem that NASA engineers had been seriously working on before.

We didn't have a rocket-powered flying space crane simmering in the background just in case we needed it.

The sky crane was conceived of and designed in response to a specific problem. They sat in a room and threw ideas around until something stuck.

And because of the particular people who sat in that particular series of meetings, the sky crane is the solution we ended up with.

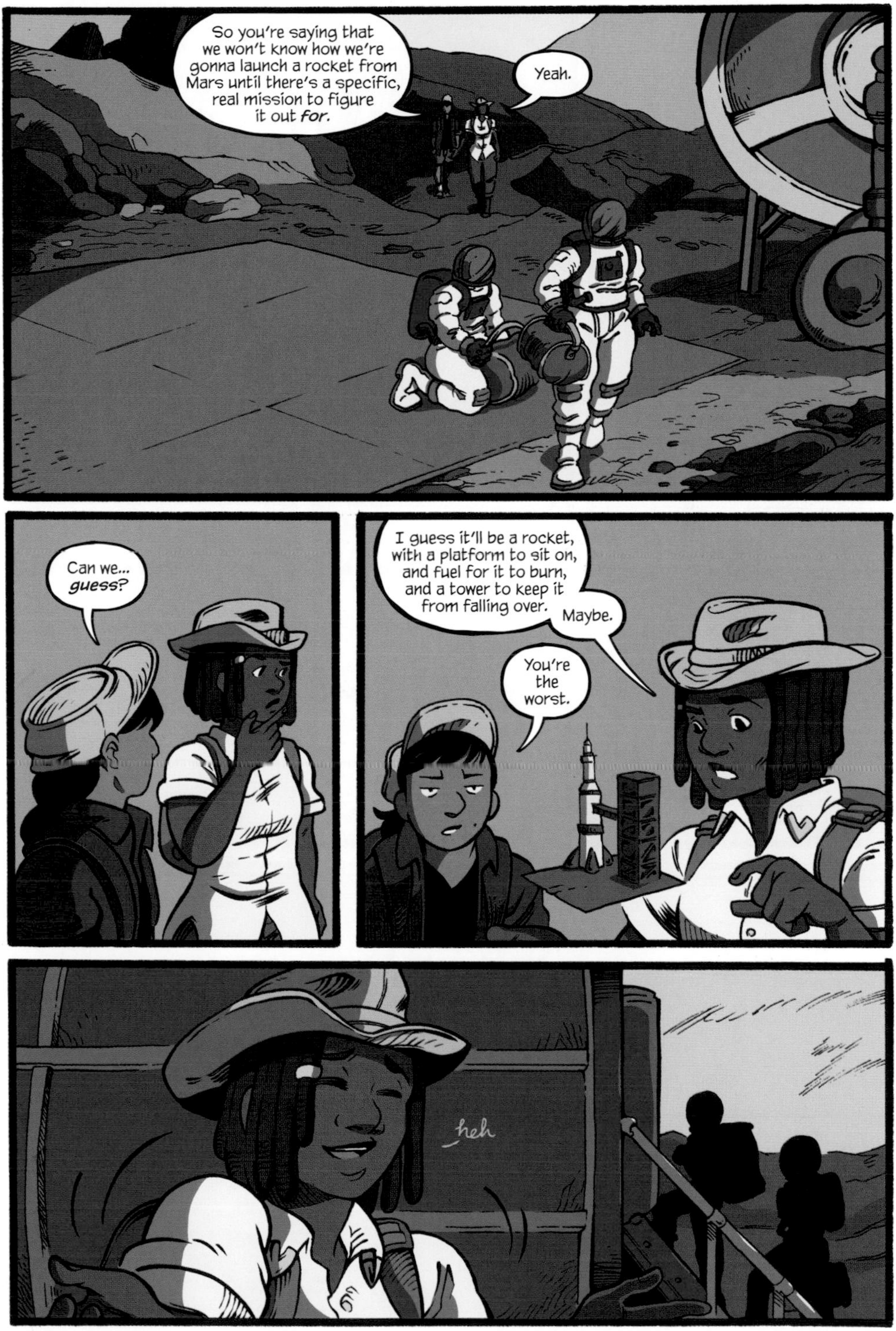
So you're saying that we won't know how we're gonna launch a rocket from Mars until there's a specific, real mission to figure it out *for.*
Yeah.
Can we... *guess?*
I guess it'll be a rocket, with a platform to sit on, and fuel for it to burn, and a tower to keep it from falling over.
Maybe.
You're the worst.
heh

All right. Enough hypotheticals.

Let's talk about the going-to-Mars plan.

Where we at?

Get me up to speed.

I... can't.

I'll understand everything you're talking about. We've just gone over every little thing, I can—

We don't have a plan.

What?

I mean... not *really*.

Eleanor, you assassin of hope and joy, *what* are you talking about?

172

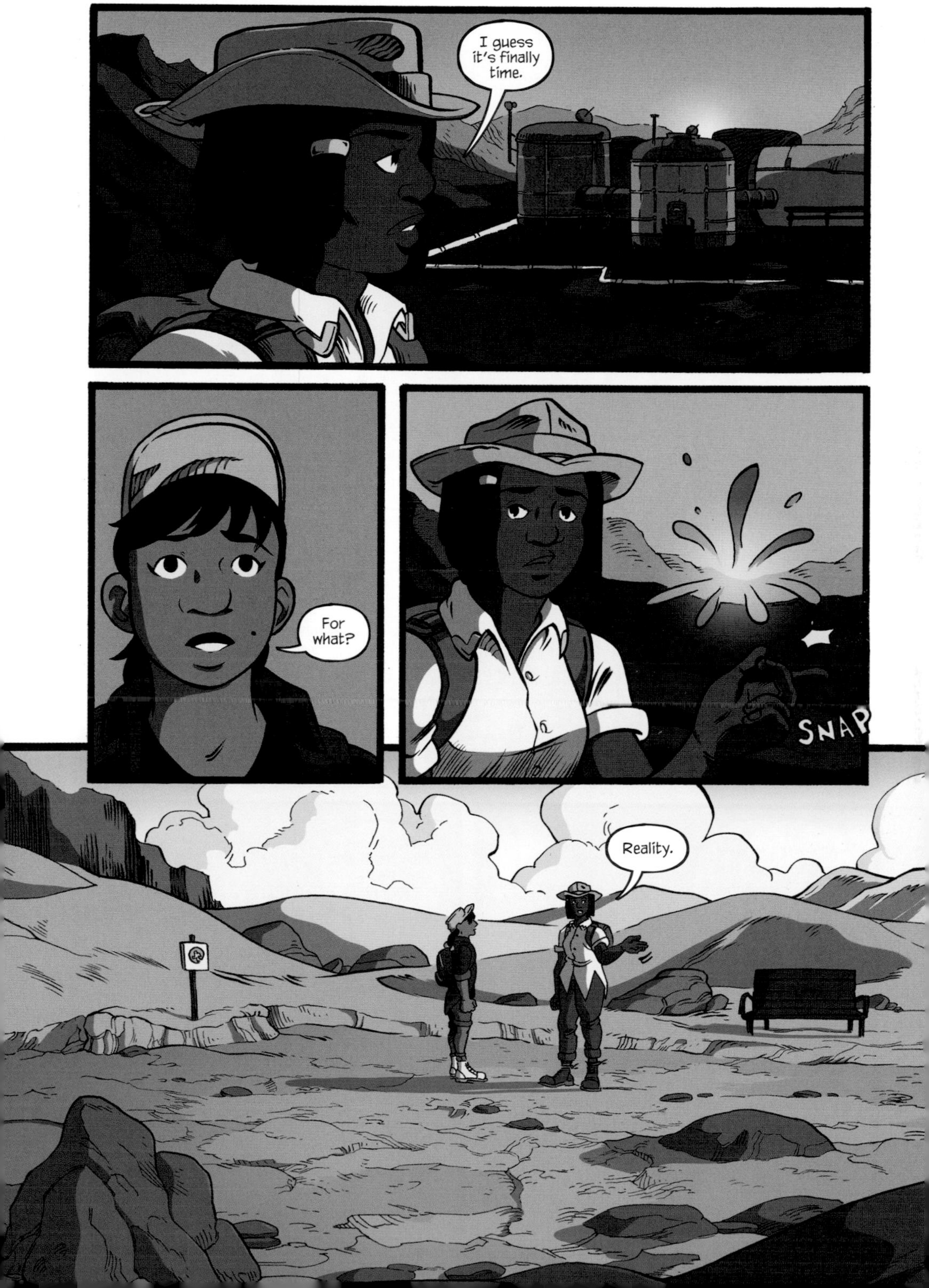
I guess it's finally time.
For what?
SNAP
Reality.

CHAPTER NINE:
MAKE IT HAPPEN

What do you mean, "reality"?

We've been talking about "reality" all day!

You asked me to tell you what's needed to send a crew to Mars.

You asked me to explain all the obstacles in the way.

And now I'm saying there's still a *huge* gap between the current state of spaceflight and a human standing on Mars.

And most of the things we'd need to bridge that gap—transit vehicles, ISRU plants, human-size Mars landers?

We haven't built them yet, and we don't really know how to.

So it'll take a while. That's fine.

You said the next good launch window is in what, 2032?

Yes.

Plenty of time!

Nadia, I hate to be like this, but we're already cutting it pretty close.

If we're going to make that launch date, we need to be working on precursor missions *now*.

Precursor?

Stepping stones across a river.

Smaller milestones that lead to where we're trying to go.

When we went to the Moon, we had a whole string of precursor missions all through the 1960s.

We launched the first person into space in 1961...

Yuri Gagarin.

Yes. And then we had to work up from there.

Longer flights in space, launching more than one person in the same vehicle, building vehicles that could travel as far as the Moon, sending a *crew* as far out as the Moon... many, many, many missions building up to Apollo 11.

Vostok 1:	First human in space. April 12, 1961.
Freedom 7:	First pilot-controlled spaceflight. May 5, 1961.
Vostok 5:	A human spends five days in space. June 14-19, 1963.
Voskhod 1:	First multiperson crew. October 12-13, 1964.
Voskhod 2:	First space walk. March 18-19, 1965.
Gemini 5:	A crew spends eight days in space. August 21-29, 1965.
Luna 9:	First spacecraft to land on the Moon intact. January 31-February 3, 1966.
Gemini 8 & ATV:	First spacecraft docking. March 16, 1966.
Luna 10:	First spacecraft to orbit the Moon. March 31-April 3, 1966.
Apollo 4:	First launch of a Saturn V rocket. November 9, 1967.
Apollo 8:	First crewed spacecraft to orbit the Moon. December 21-27, 1968.
Apollo 11:	First humans to land on the Moon. July 16-24, 1969.

And look, the pace of progress back then was buckwild—we call it the "space race" for a reason.

But it still took humanity eight years to get from Gagarin to boots on the Moon.

Fine.

But then the Moon landings must be a precursor for Mars, right?

I'd say so.

The Apollo astronauts are the only humans who've stood on anything like another planet.

What about the Mars rovers, like *Curiosity*?

Yes, you could say those are precursors.

They've all taught us something about the planet, how to land on it, what the surface is like.

And space stations?

Definitely.

They taught us how to live in space for more than a few days at a time, how to assemble a large habitat in orbit, and how to keep that habitat operating continuously.

And we're working on new rockets, aren't we? NASA's SLS and the SpaceX BFR.

True.

And we're sending another rover. We're doing *plenty* of stuff.

Yes, but...

There's a *huge* gap between a robot car and a lander full of people.

And if we want to close that gap, we need to get some pretty ambitious projects in the spaceflight pipeline.

Soon.

Okay, but we *have*?

Like, SpaceX was talking about sending people to Mars in the 2020s.

Yes, I *know* it's not likely—they can't design and build and test all the stuff we talked about in just a few years.

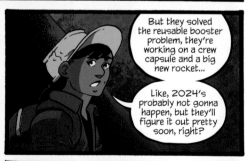

But they solved the reusable booster problem, they're working on a crew capsule and a big new rocket...

Like, 2024's probably not gonna happen, but they'll figure it out pretty soon, right?

Maybe.

Can't you let me have this one thing?

Listen, Nadia...

Private companies like SpaceX and Blue Origin are building and launching variations on the kinds of rockets we've already flown. New designs, some great new capabilities, but in a lot of ways we're behind where we were in the Apollo era.

If we want to go to Mars, we'll have to build the largest rocket in history. And that's just the launch vehicle. That doesn't solve any of the other problems you and I talked about today.

Let's say we *do* somehow have an interplanetary rocket that's ready to send cargo to Mars in 2032. What equipment would we even put in it?

All right, fine. We've got a long way to go, I get it.

So. What do we need to do next?

That depends on who you ask.

Some people think we should focus on long-term habitats in cislunar space—still inside the Moon's orbit, but much farther away than the space station is. It'd be good practice for a Mars transit vehicle.

Some people think we should start with finding new, more sustainable ways of going to the Moon.

Some people think we should be aiming for a crewed Mars flyby mission, or maybe land on one of the little Martian moons, Phobos and Deimos—they're so small they hardly have any gravity, much easier to deal with than a whole big planet.

Whatever path we take, if we want to hit that 2032 launch window? We need to get started very soon.

Yeah, but that's a decade from now. We have plenty of time!

The Mars 2020 rover was announced in 2012. Eight years from announcement to launch, for a mission that's only an upgrade of *Curiosity*.

Ellie, you *just said...*

We went from first-dude-in-space to *landing on the Moon* in eight years.

Yeah, and that was a terrible idea.

Space is hard, and a lot can go wrong. In all the excitement of progress, it's easy to forget about how important it is to be sure you know what you're doing.

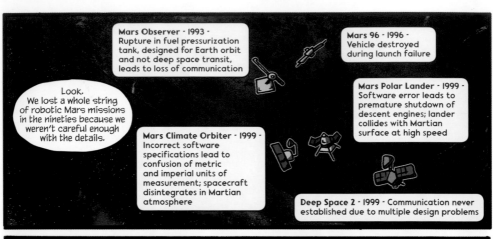

Mars Observer · 1993 · Rupture in fuel pressurization tank, designed for Earth orbit and not deep space transit, leads to loss of communication

Mars 96 · 1996 · Vehicle destroyed during launch failure

Look. We lost a whole string of robotic Mars missions in the nineties because we weren't careful enough with the details.

Mars Polar Lander · 1999 · Software error leads to premature shutdown of descent engines; lander collides with Martian surface at high speed

Mars Climate Orbiter · 1999 · Incorrect software specifications lead to confusion of metric and imperial units of measurement; spacecraft disintegrates in Martian atmosphere

Deep Space 2 · 1999 · Communication never established due to multiple design problems

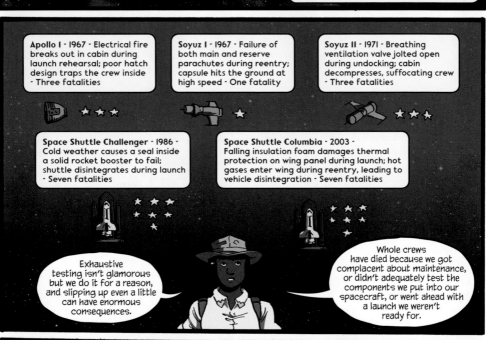

Apollo 1 · 1967 · Electrical fire breaks out in cabin during launch rehearsal; poor hatch design traps the crew inside · Three fatalities

Soyuz 1 · 1967 · Failure of both main and reserve parachutes during reentry; capsule hits the ground at high speed · One fatality

Soyuz 11 · 1971 · Breathing ventilation valve jolted open during undocking; cabin decompresses, suffocating crew · Three fatalities

Space Shuttle Challenger · 1986 · Cold weather causes a seal inside a solid rocket booster to fail; shuttle disintegrates during launch · Seven fatalities

Space Shuttle Columbia · 2003 · Falling insulation foam damages thermal protection on wing panel during launch; hot gases enter wing during reentry, leading to vehicle disintegration · Seven fatalities

Exhaustive testing isn't glamorous but we do it for a reason, and slipping up even a little can have enormous consequences.

Whole crews have died because we got complacent about maintenance, or didn't adequately test the components we put into our spacecraft, or went ahead with a launch we weren't ready for.

Listen, Nadia...

I want boots on Mars more than anyone. But I want to do it the right way.

Human spaceflight is complicated and dangerous.

You can't rush these things.

182

And keep in mind, seriously, Mars is *far!* *Away!* Every precursor mission to Mars will take *multiple years* from start to finish. If we're going to do this...there are realities to the schedule that we just can't get around.

Is there a robotic sample return mission in the works? Are we designing a transit vehicle in earnest? Has there been an announcement of a crewed flyby of Mars? Heck, have we scheduled even one launch that'll send a human being out of low Earth orbit?

...No?

No. And if we're going to send humans to Mars in the next couple decades, we need to be doing all of those things *today.*

"Commercial Crew" programs are just getting off the ground. And as for public programs, well, we're not in the Cold War anymore. Convincing a modern government to make the political and financial commitments necessary to take on a problem as complicated and expensive as going to Mars is going to be...

Nadia.

I'm sorry, I...

It's fine.

It's *fine*, I just...

I really *care* about this, okay? I've been dreaming about Mars for my entire life.

And I came here today so you could help me get there.

And you're basically telling me that it's not going to happen.

No! No, I don't...

Nadia, that's not what I meant at all!

I *absolutely* think we can get to Mars. That's why I'm *here*.

That's why I'm talking to you! You *specifically*, the person who actually wants to go!

I just...I want to arm you with as much information as I can. I want to give you the best possible chance to make this happen.

Then tell me what to *do*.

Like me *personally*.

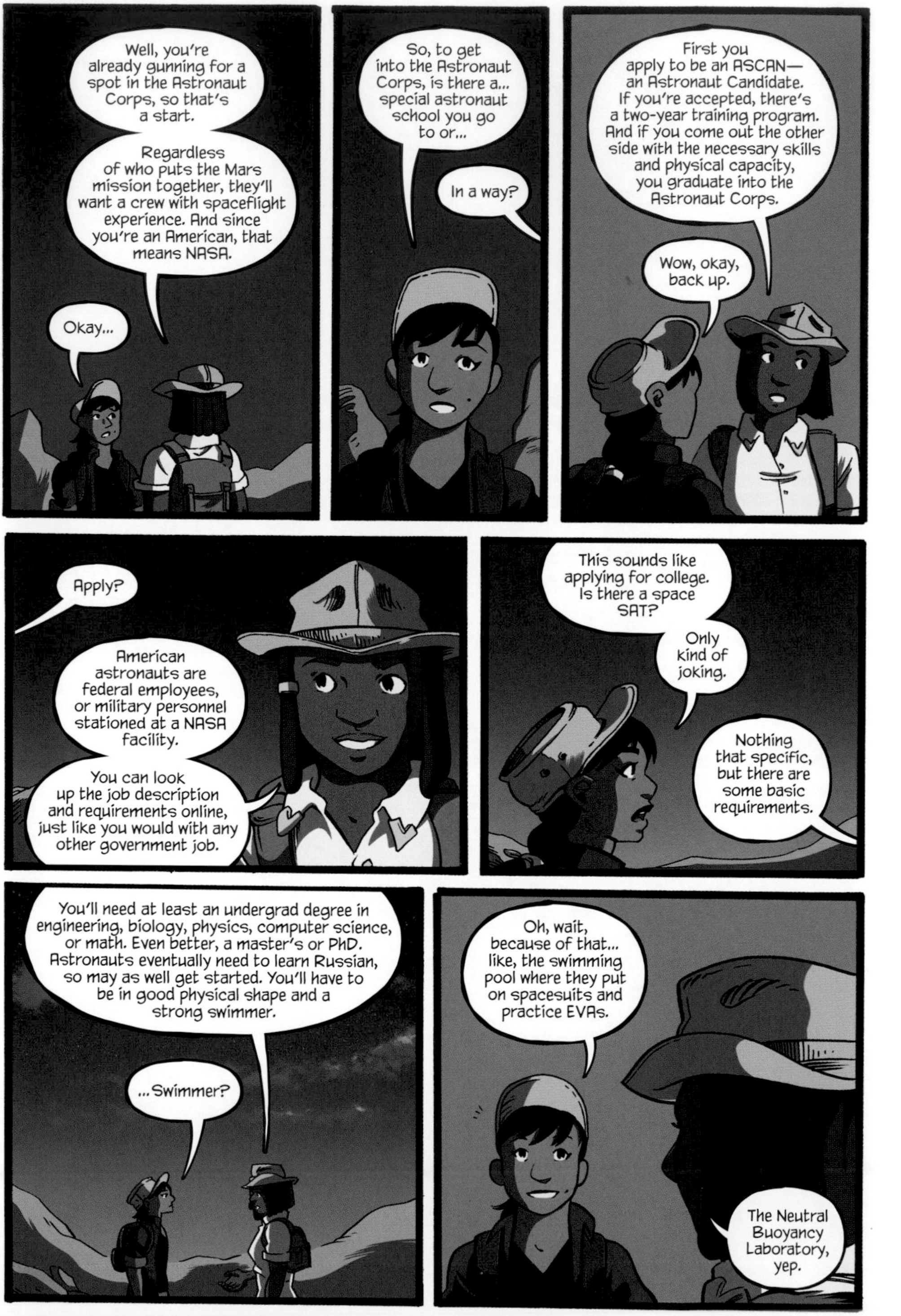
Well, you're already gunning for a spot in the Astronaut Corps, so that's a start.
Regardless of who puts the Mars mission together, they'll want a crew with spaceflight experience. And since you're an American, that means NASA.
Okay...
So, to get into the Astronaut Corps, is there a... special astronaut school you go to or...
In a way?
First you apply to be an ASCAN—an Astronaut Candidate. If you're accepted, there's a two-year training program. And if you come out the other side with the necessary skills and physical capacity, you graduate into the Astronaut Corps.
Wow, okay, back up.
Apply?
American astronauts are federal employees, or military personnel stationed at a NASA facility.
You can look up the job description and requirements online, just like you would with any other government job.
This sounds like applying for college. Is there a space SAT?
Only kind of joking.
Nothing that specific, but there are some basic requirements.
You'll need at least an undergrad degree in engineering, biology, physics, computer science, or math. Even better, a master's or PhD. Astronauts eventually need to learn Russian, so may as well get started. You'll have to be in good physical shape and a strong swimmer.
...Swimmer?
Oh, wait, because of that... like, the swimming pool where they put on spacesuits and practice EVAs.
The Neutral Buoyancy Laboratory, yep.

Now, do keep in mind that ASCAN classes are only put together a couple times a decade, and they're usually pretty small—the largest to date had only thirty-five people.

I personally think you'd be the perfect choice for the first Mars mission, but *alas*, it's not up to me.

Boo.

So while you're choosing what you want to study and what kind of work you want to do after school, make sure it's something you genuinely enjoy.

And remember that even if you don't make it all the way to the Astronaut Corps, there are *many* people who work on the ground to make space exploration happen.

Like you.

Yes. Like me.

But seriously, apply.

They're explicitly looking for women and people of color in their astronaut classes. They want people who are passionate about spaceflight and science and exploration.

You're an absolutely ideal applicant, and I hope you try.

And in the meantime, while you're aiming at that ASCAN spot? Vote. Write to your congresspeople.

Ellie, come on.

I'm serious.

Private spaceflight isn't something you can do much about one way or the other. And right now, practically speaking, exploration is funded by governments.

So tell your government that space is important to you. Send letters. Make phone calls. Visit their offices, if you're up for it.

None of those people care what I think.

You're be surprised. Politicians are still *people*.

And then *vote*. Pay attention to who's supporting the sciences, and show up to the polls to help keep them in office.

You're making this sound like it's... just normal business.

It *is*.

That's the whole point of everything I've told you today. Mars is a difficult goal to aim for, but it is *absolutely* possible. If we commit, if we put in the money and the time... Nadia, there's *no reason* that we can't get you there.

You think that a human being is going to stand on Mars while you're alive to see it.

Absolutely.

You think we're gonna build all this stuff we talked about.

Sort of.

Look. When we talked about building space stations back in the 1950s, people like Wernher von Braun came up with these sleek, gorgeous designs. Shining silver wheels in orbit with simulated gravity.

What we got is a chain of cans and trusses.

An orbiting jumble of compromises.

But you know what?

It's *up there.*

We *did it.*

We got *fifteen* countries to work with each other over decades of time to build a freakin' *space station* that human beings actually *live* in!

That's a *huge deal!*

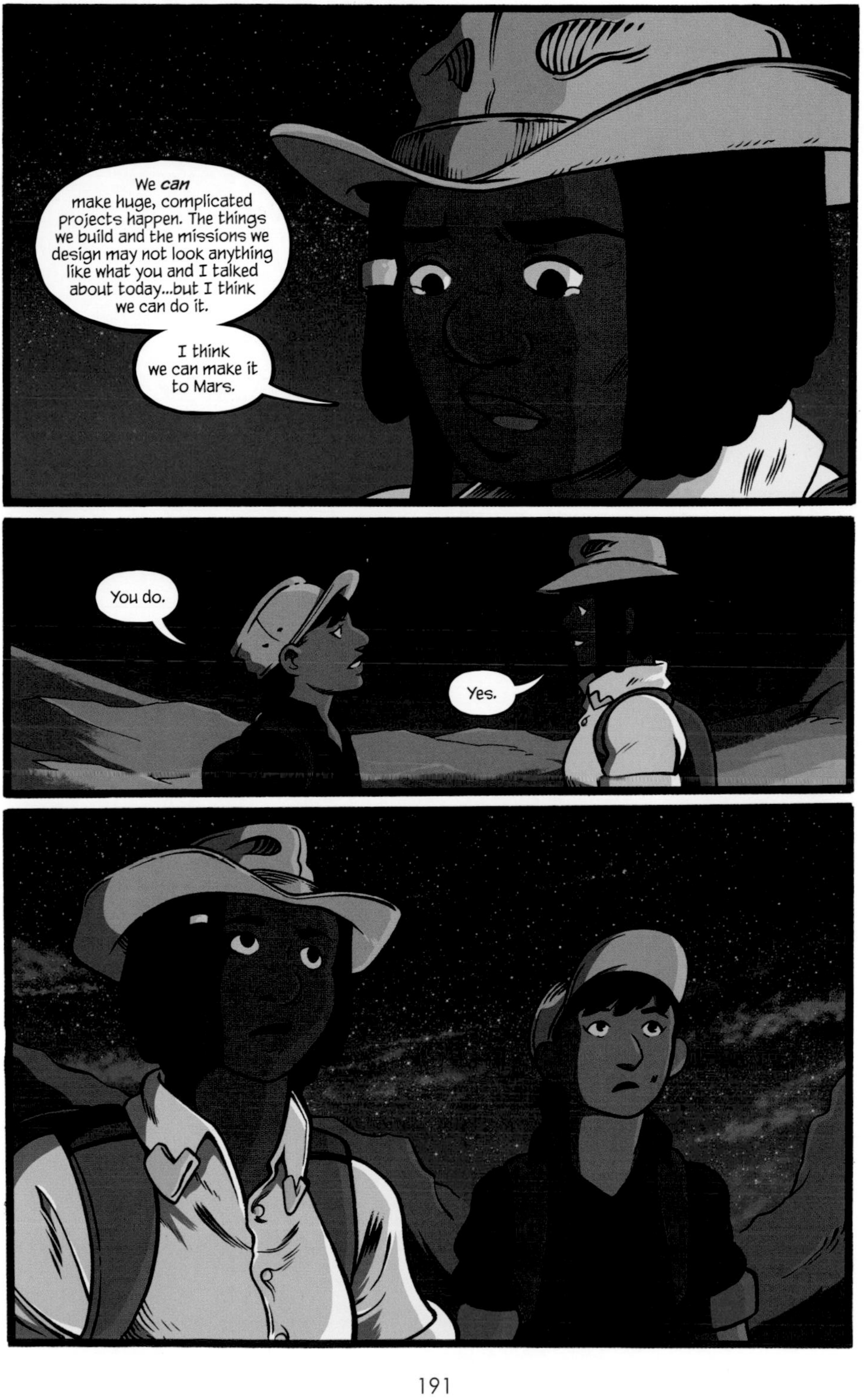
We *can* make huge, complicated projects happen. The things we build and the missions we design may not look anything like what you and I talked about today...but I think we can do it.
I think we can make it to Mars.
You do.
Yes.

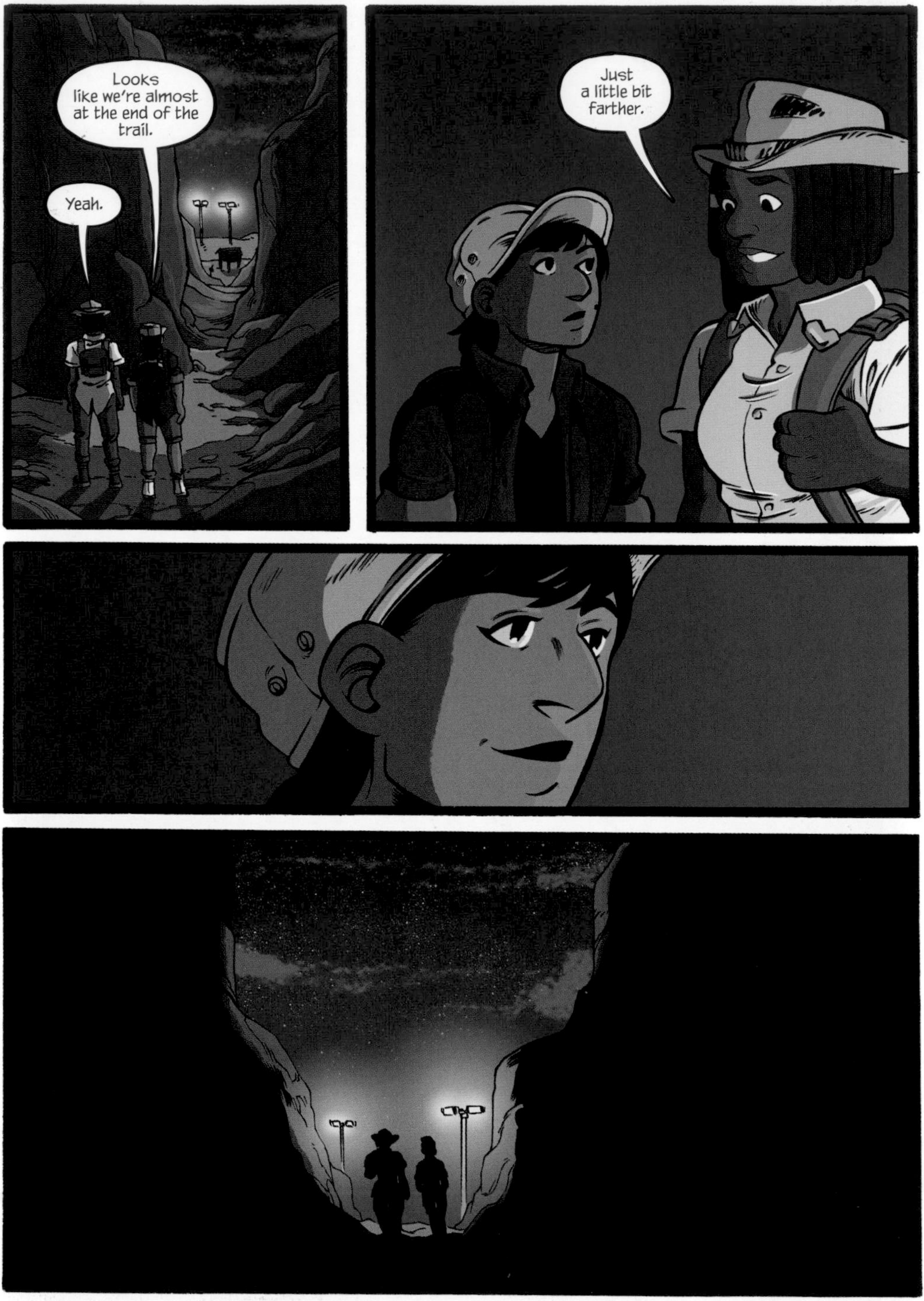
Looks like we're almost at the end of the trail.
Yeah.
Just a little bit farther.

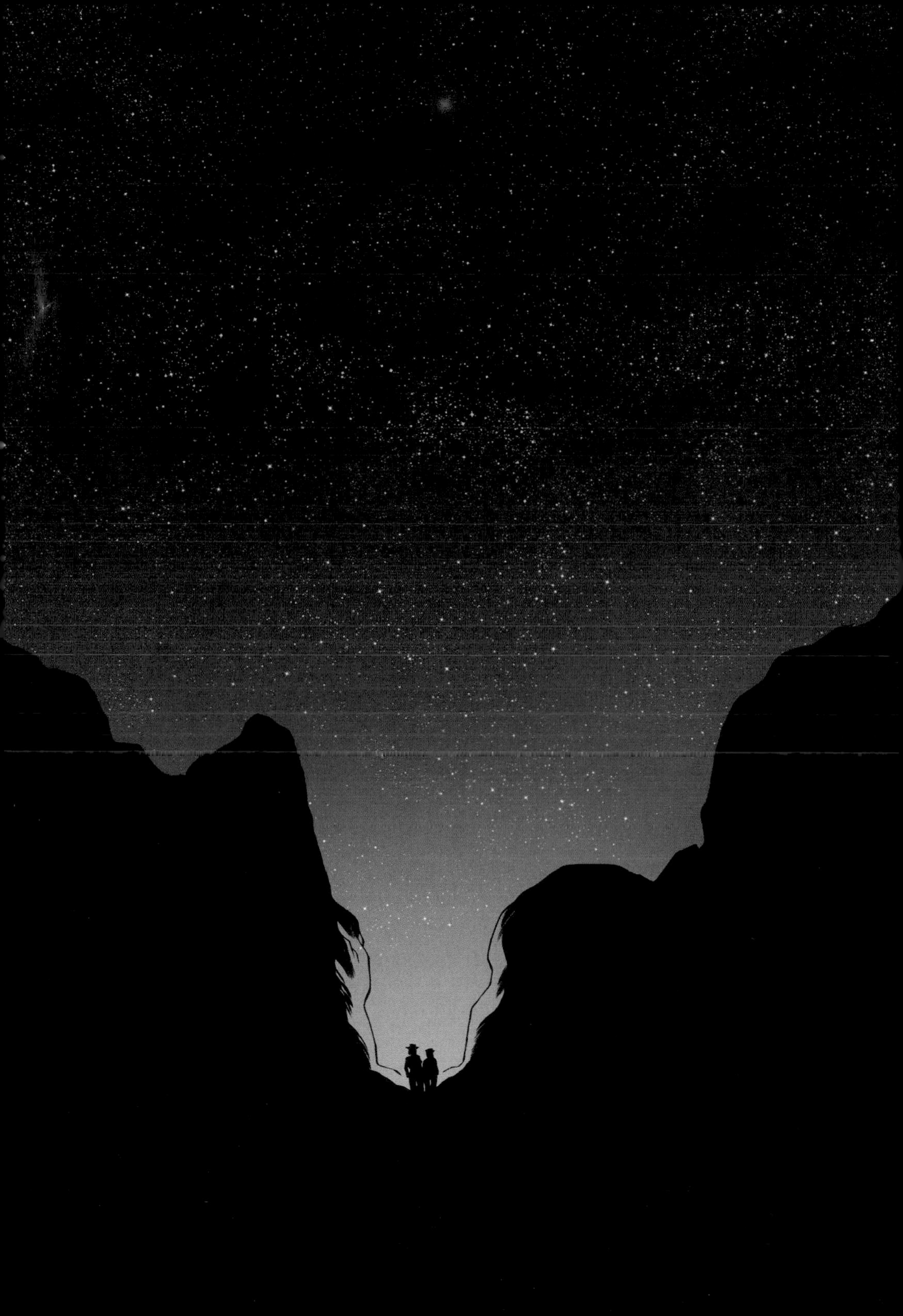

Research and Resources

My goal when writing *The Mars Challenge* was to give readers a broad survey of the principles of human spaceflight and the current state of space exploration, which meant I had a lot of work to do in order to deepen my own understanding of these things. The research for this book took place over multiple years and involved more sources than I could possibly list in these pages. But here are some key informational avenues I went down over the course of making *The Mars Challenge*.

—Alison

NASA Socials

nasa.gov/connect/social

These are free-to-the-public outreach events run by NASA. You sign up as a potential attendee, and if you're selected you're responsible for getting yourself to the NASA facility where the event will take place. After that, NASA employees will take care of you and your group for as little as a couple of hours or as long as a couple of days. Events are often based around a specific mission, and the longer ones involve getting onto a bus and being driven around the facility to see space exploration infrastructure, meet scientists and support staff, and attend lectures on the science and engineering principles behind current and upcoming NASA missions. To date, I've participated in four NASA Socials: a talk by astronaut Joseph M. Acaba at NASA Headquarters in Washington, DC; the launch of the TDRS-K communications satellite at the Kennedy Space Center; a deep dive into space station science at the Johnson Space Center; and the launch of the Orion EFT-I prototype crew capsule at Kennedy Space Center. (The NASA Social at Johnson was where I was able to walk around the space station mockup featured in this book!)

NASA Budget Requests

nasa.gov/news/budget

These are massive documents that NASA assembles annually as a resource for Congress and that are available for the public to read online. A NASA Budget Request is exactly what it says on the tin: It lays out the funding that NASA will require for the next fiscal year. Every mission currently in the pipeline is explained, as well as all ongoing operating expenses for NASA programs and infrastructure. Because most members of Congress are laypeople when it comes to space exploration, the budget requests are easy to read and understand and offer a comprehensible and complete view of the current state of all space exploration connected to the US government. These documents are amazing windows into the long-term planning that lies behind space exploration programs, and I used them to track individual missions over time. Early drafts of *The Mars Challenge* included a play-by-play of MSL *Curiosity*'s journey from proposal to an operational rover on Mars, which involved combing through twelve years of Budget Requests.

NASA Technical Reports Server

ntrs.nasa.gov

From the perspective of an outsider such as myself, this is a chaotic gold mine of a website. You can search through an archive of thousands of documents from the entire history of NASA and download PDFs ranging from presentations on life-support system corrosion to user manuals for the International Space Station. I spent weeks plugging in keywords to see what I could fish from the depths. Readability and relevance varied, but overall the NTRS was an absolute treasure, and I highly encourage you to go and poke around.

NASA Websites

nasa.gov

NASA.gov and its many subsites are dense with useful information about current missions, aerospace infrastructure, and planetary science. These sites have had multiple overhauls and redesigns over the years, and in the process older mission pages are often orphaned—their designs static and their content no longer linked to. However, these pages are still indexed by search engines, and often the orphaned subsites are still internally functional. I made extensive use of these hidden NASA web pages, particularly when researching older missions like the Mars Exploration Rovers, the space shuttle program, or the early years of the International Space Station.

Wikipedia

wikipedia.org

Space enthusiasts take the topic very seriously and chip in to maintain community resources, and so the relevant sections of Wikipedia are thorough and reliable. This was a fantastic resource for hunting down technical information about vehicles, explanations of physics principles, mission timelines, and key dates in the history of space exploration. As with any source, it's best to double-check with another reputable text on the topic, but if you want to go down some spaceflight rabbit holes, Wikipedia is a fantastic place to start.

Humans to Mars Summit

h2m.exploremars.org

This is an annual conference in Washington, DC, where experts give talks on the current state of human spaceflight and the many possible roads toward a crewed mission to Mars. I watched hours of lectures remotely and attended myself in 2014. This event was particularly helpful as a foundation because of its focus and breadth—there were talks on analog missions, on types of engines, on Martian planetary science, on possible trajectories and mission architectures, and much more.

Space Exploration Alliance Legislative Blitz

spaceexplorationalliance.org/blitz

Every year, representatives from multiple space exploration advocacy groups gather in Washington, DC, organize into groups of two to four people, and spend two days in meetings with members of Congress. Participants are private citizens with a personal interest in space exploration, and the goal is to make the case in person for continuing to fund the future of both human and robotic space exploration. I participated in the blitz for two years, and spoke to dozens of senators, representatives, and congressional staffers about how important NASA is to me. I came away with a much better understanding of how space exploration policy moves through the mechanisms of the US government.

Early character designs by Wyeth Yates

Glossary

acceleration	The rate of change of an object's velocity over time. An object's acceleration is the net result of all forces acting upon it.
aerobraking	Flying a spacecraft through a planet's atmosphere in order to slow it down, and therefore lower its orbit.
aerospace	A blanket term for the study and practice of flying in Earth's atmosphere or in space.
air lock	A device that allows people and objects to pass in and out of a sealed chamber that has a different air pressure than the space surrounding it, while minimizing the effect on the air pressure of that sealed chamber. Astronauts conducting spacewalks use an air lock to come and go from the International Space Station.
analog mission	Simulated missions of human space exploration, conducted on Earth in environments that replicate the extreme conditions and/or isolation of another planet.
analog study	Scientific studies that replicate some aspect of the effects of human spaceflight on the body, in order to better understand how living in space impacts human beings and to test countermeasures for known health problems.
Apollo Program	A human spaceflight program carried out by NASA between 1961 and 1972, which resulted in the first crewed orbit of the moon in May 1969 and the first crewed moon landing in July 1969.
ASCAN	See "Astronaut Candidate."
astronaut	A person who is trained by a human spaceflight program to serve as a crew member of a spacecraft.
Astronaut Candidate	A person who has been selected by NASA for training as a potential candidate for the Astronaut Corps.
Astronaut Corps	A program within NASA that selects and trains astronauts and that provides them as crew members for missions.
atmosphere	A layer of gases surrounding a planet that is held in place by the gravity of that planet.
atmospheric pressure	The force with which atmosphere is pushing on objects within it.

Blue Origin A privately funded manufacturer of aerospace vehicles, based in the United States.

brine Water with a high salt content.

burn The use of propulsion systems to change the velocity of a spacecraft.

Canadarm2 A robotic arm mounted on the International Space Station, which is used to move equipment and supplies outside the station, to provide a platform for working astronauts and to service instruments and payloads attached to the station. The Canadarm2 played a key role in assembling the station itself. Also known as the "Mobile Servicing System."

capsule A spacecraft that is designed to reenter the Earth's atmosphere without wings. A common design for crewed spacecraft.

carbon dioxide A colorless gas that aerobic organisms—including humans—exhale as a by-product of respiration. Too much carbon dioxide in the air can cause suffocation. Often abbreviated as CO_2.

cargo Objects transported by a large vehicle. In the context of spaceflight, food, water, equipment, experiments, etc., could all be classified as cargo.

centrifugal force A force that accelerates objects in a rotating device away from the axis of rotation.

chemical propulsion Propulsion in which thrust is provided as the result of a chemical reaction.

circulate To move or cause to move through a closed system or space.

cislunar Between the Earth and the moon.

closed-loop life support An ideal system—self-contained and self-reliant—for keeping humans alive in a hostile environment such as space. Earth itself is currently the only known closed-loop life-support system.

CNSA China National Space Administration, the national space agency of China.

commercial crew A program in which NASA partners with private aerospace companies. The goal is to fly astronauts to the International Space Station using privately operated crew vehicles.

consumable	Goods that are intended to be consumed and that are finite. Food, water, and oxygen are consumables in human spaceflight.
coronal mass ejection	A significant eruption of plasma from the surface of the sun.
cosmic ray	A form of high-energy radiation that originates from outside of the solar system.
cosmonaut	A term used by the Russian Space Agency to refer to members of its crewed spaceflight program.
crew	The group of people assigned to board and operate a vehicle.
cruise stage	The configuration of a spacecraft for travel between Earth and its destination.
CSA	Canadian Space Agency, the national space agency of Canada.
cupola	A module of the International Space Station designed for observation of the Earth and of the station's exterior, built by the ESA.
Curiosity	See "Mars Science Laboratory."
decelerate	To reduce or cause to reduce the velocity of an object.
decompression	A reduction in air pressure.
deep space	Space outside of the moon's orbit.
delta velocity	A measure of the energy needed to perform a spacecraft maneuver. Often abbreviated as "delta-v."
Destiny	A module of the International Space Station designed for conducting research, built by NASA. Also known as the "U.S. Lab."
ECLSS	See "Environmental Control and Life Support System."
ecosystem	A community of living organisms interacting with nonliving parts of their environment as part of a system.
EDL	Stands for Entry, Descent, and Landing—the transition of a vehicle from space to a planet's surface.
EMU	See "Extravehicular Mobility Unit."

Environmental Control and Life Support System	A system on board the International Space Station that keeps the vehicle habitable by humans. It provides or controls atmospheric pressure, breathable air, fire detection/suppression, waste management, and water.
ESA	European Space Agency, a space exploration organization with twenty-two member states.
EVA	See "extravehicular activity."
extravehicular activity	Any activity conducted by an astronaut or cosmonaut outside of their vehicle. Often referred to as a "spacewalk."
Extravehicular Mobility Unit	A pressurized and insulated garment that allows an astronaut to survive outside of their vehicle in space. Often called a "space suit."
faring	A protective nose cone around the payload on top of a rocket.
fines	Soil or regolith made up of very fine particles.
fire	To activate a vehicle's engines.
flight heritage	A history of real-world use for an aerospace vehicle or component.
g	A unit used to express the stresses on a person or vehicle during flight. One "g" feels subjectively like the force of gravity one experiences standing on the Earth's surface.
gravity	The force by which objects are drawn toward the center of a planet, star, or other body.
gravity well	A way to visualize the gravitational field surrounding an object in space—the more massive the body, the stronger its gravitational field, and the deeper the gravity well.
ground	Shorthand for the team of support staff on Earth who help to operate, monitor, and maintain vehicles in space.
habitat	A structure on the surface of a planet other than Earth in which humans reside.
heat shield	A component of a spacecraft that protects it from the heat generated when it enters a planet's atmosphere.
human-rated	When a vehicle has been certified as capable of safely transporting humans.
hydrazine	A monopropellant used in some spacecraft. Highly toxic.

In-Situ Resource Utilization	Processing locally available resources to provide consumables for use in a mission, such as water, fuel, or oxygen.
infrastructure	The physical and administrative facilities and resources that support a given organization or endeavor, such as human spaceflight.
International Space Station	A space station in low Earth orbit, built from smaller modules and continuously inhabited since 2000. The Space Station is a joint endeavor between five space agencies: NASA, Roscosmos, JAXA, ESA, and CSA.
interplanetary	Located or traveling between planets.
ion propulsion	Ion engines use electricity to expel plasma through a nozzle, which generates thrust. The electricity is usually generated by solar panels.
ionizing radiation	Subatomic particles moving at high speeds and with enough energy to detach electrons from atoms and molecules, which ionizes them.
ISRU	See "In-Situ Resource Utilization."
JAXA	Japanese Aerospace Exploration Agency, the national space agency of Japan.
Lagrangian point	A point between two large bodies in space where a smaller object will maintain its position relative to them if left alone.
lander	A vehicle designed to land on the surface of a planet.
launch	A flight that reaches space.
launch facility	The structures, resources, and support staff that allow vehicles to be launched into space.
launchpad	A structure from which a rocket-propelled vehicle is vertically launched.
launch vehicle	A vehicle, usually rocket-propelled, which is used to carry a payload into space.
launch window	The time period within which a specific mission must be launched.
life support	The collection of systems that allows humans to inhabit otherwise hostile or deadly environments.
low Earth orbit	An Earth-centered orbit with an altitude between 180 and 2,000 kilometers (112 to 1,243 miles).

lunar	Having to do with Earth's moon.
magnetic field	A way to visualize the shape of magnetic forces in the space around an object that generates them, such as Earth.
magnetosphere	A region of space around a planet in which charged particles are affected by that planet's magnetic field.
Mars Exploration Rover	One of two robotic exploration rovers that were launched in 2003 and landed on Mars in 2004. Informally named *Spirit* and *Opportunity*.
Mars Science Laboratory	A robotic exploration rover that was launched in 2011 and landed on Mars in 2012. Informally named *Curiosity*.
mass	A measure of the substance of an object—how much "stuff" it is made out of.
microgravity	Very weak gravity, as experienced aboard a spacecraft in orbit.
milestone	A significant event or stage of development.
Mir	A space station that flew in low Earth orbit from 1986 until 2001, operated first by the Soviet Union and then by Russia.
mission	A specific aerospace task such as operating a robotic rover or launching a new crew to the International Space Station.
Mobile Launcher Platform	A two-story structure used at the Kennedy Space Center as a way to transport vehicles to the launch pad and also as a platform from which the vehicles are launched.
module	A discrete section of a spacecraft, usually designed to connect with other modules in order to operate as part of a larger vehicle.
monopropellant	Chemical fuel that releases the energy stored in its molecular bonds when a catalyst causes it to break down.
NASA	National Aeronautics and Space Administration, the national space agency of the United States.
nozzle	A device that controls the direction or characteristics of how a fluid or gas flows as it exits a chamber or pipe.
nuclear thermal propulsion	An engine which uses the heat from a nuclear reaction to heat a fluid such as liquid hydrogen, which then expands through a nozzle to create thrust.

Opportunity	One of the two Mars Exploration Rovers.
orbit	The path of an object through space around a planet or star, curved into a circle or an ellipse by gravity.
orbital insertion	The process of changing a spacecraft's acceleration such that it can enter a stable orbit around a planet.
oxygen	A chemical that many living things require to survive, including humans. It is naturally generated by plants via photosynthesis and can be artificially generated by breaking water down into hydrogen and oxygen using electrolysis.
particle	A very small bit of mass.
payload	The spacecraft or satellite that a launch vehicle is carrying into space.
plant	Short for "physical plant" or "mechanical plant," a part of the infrastructure that is needed to operate and/or maintain a given facility.
precursor mission	A mission designed as a stepping stone to another more complex, challenging, dangerous, and/or expensive mission. Often these missions are a real-world test of a key technology or process.
pressurized	Sealed and containing air; in spaceflight, this usually refers to the level of air pressure that humans need to live.
propellant	A substance used to create propulsion.
propulsion	The action or process of pushing an object forward.
rack	A standardized frame for holding discrete systems or experiments on board a spacecraft. May also be used to refer to the system that has been secured on the rack.
radiation	The emission of energy in the form of particles or waves.
radiator	A heat exchange built to transfer thermal energy, used in heating or cooling.
regolith	The layer of rocky material that covers solid bedrock.
resupply	To provide with fresh consumables and other resources that have been depleted.
retropropulsion	A method for decelerating a vehicle, wherein an engine is fired in the direction of travel.
retrorocket	A rocket engine used for retropropulsion.

robotic exploration	Using uncrewed spacecraft or rovers to gather information about space or planetary bodies.
Roscosmos	The Roscosmos State Corporation for Space Activities, the national space agency of Russia.
rover	A vehicle designed to move across the surface of a planet for the purposes of exploration.
satellite	An uncrewed object that has been launched into orbit around a planet.
Saturn V	A series of NASA rockets that were designed for the Apollo program and that carried human beings to the moon. To date, the Saturn V is the only rocket to have launched a crewed spacecraft out of low Earth orbit. The final Saturn V launch was in 1973.
shirt-sleeve environment	A pressurized compartment in a vehicle where no protective clothing is needed.
sky crane	A mechanism that lowered the Mars Science Laboratory from a rocket-powered descent stage to the ground, providing a soft landing.
solar	Having to do with the sun.
solar electric propulsion	A propulsion system that uses solar panels as an energy source. Usually an ion drive.
solar flare	A large eruption of electromagnetic radiation from the surface of the sun, accompanied by a flash of increased brightness. Large flares are often also accompanied by a coronal mass ejection.
solar power	The conversion of sunlight into electricity.
solar system	The system of planets and other objects in orbit around a central star.
solar wind	The flow of charged particles from the sun.
Soyuz	A series of crewed spacecraft designed by the Soviet space program and now in use by Roscosmos. "Soyuz" may also refer to the rockets that launch these spacecraft. As of this writing, the Soyuz is the only human-rated spacecraft in use that can carry a crew into orbit.
space golf cart	A golf cart . . . but in space.

space shuttle	A partially reusable crewed spacecraft system that was operated by NASA between 1981 and 2011. It could carry cargo and crew to low Earth orbit, and its payloads included the Hubble Space Telescope and multiple components of the International Space Station.
space station	See "International Space Station."
space suit	See "Extravehicular Mobility Unit."
SpaceX	A privately funded manufacturer of aerospace vehicles, based in the United States.
spacecraft	A vehicle or a machine designed to operate in space.
spacewalk	See "extravehicular activity."
Spirit	One of the two Mars Exploration Rovers.
stage	A section of a rocket that has its own fuel and engine and that is discarded once the fuel has run out.
supersonic	Traveling faster than the speed of sound.
surface suit	A pressurized and insulated protective suit meant to be worn while on the surface of a planet that can't support human life.
system	A set of things all working together and/or interacting with one another.
trajectory	The path a spacecraft will take to a given destination.
Tranquility	A module of the International Space Station which contains life support systems, environmental control systems, and exercise equipment. Built by NASA; also known as "Node 3."
transit	The period when a spacecraft is moving from its origin to its destination.
transit vehicle	A spacecraft in which a crew travels from Earth orbit to another planet.
vehicle	A machine used to transport people, cargo, or other machines.
velocity	An object's rate and direction of motion.
waste	Unwanted or unusable material, often left over from other processes.

Acknowledgments

Alison would like to thank . . .

The entire team at First Second Books, but most especially: Calista Brill for asking me if I'd like to write a comic about space, and for helping me shape the kind of book *The Mars Challenge* was going to be; Robyn Chapman for getting me from a huge messy outline to the actual book you're holding in your hands; Hazel Newlevant for jumping on board for the final stretch of Getting This Thing Out The Door; and Kirk Benshoff, Molly Johanson, and Andrew Arnold for their fantastic design work.

Superstar agent Eddie Schnieder, and the indomitable Jabberwocky crew.

Our brilliant and invaluable expert readers, Emily Lakdawalla and Liz Warren.

The many, many people who organized and facilitated the NASA Social events which I attended, and the hundreds of nerds who went on those adventures with me.

Rick Zucker and the rest of the team who organize the Space Exploration Alliance Legislative Blitz, as well as the gentlemen who Blitzed with me the two years I was able to participate. It was an honor and a pleasure to make awkward conversation with congressional staffers with you.

Everyone at the Planetary Society, but particularly Casey Dreier, who once took the time to explain the finer details of Space Policy over drinks in a Washington, DC, train station.

My friend and collaborator Wyeth Yates, for drawing a staggering number of very cool rockets, for being patient with endless nitpicky revisions, and for bringing Eleanor and Nadia to life.

Wyeth would like to thank . . .

Kristin, Chip, Caitlin, and Jay, without whose support, guidance, love and sense of humor, this book literally would not exist. To Ali Wilgus, Robyn Chapman, Hazel Newlevant, and the team at First Second for trusting me with an incredible script and helping me through the process of making this book. To Kendra, for always being there to crack me up when I needed it. To Cheryl, who has learned a lot more about space travel and comics than she probably wanted to know.

To the Weirfield, Tompkins, Lafayette, and Corner Grind crews. You know who you are, and I love you all very dearly. To Ishiii and The Long Rests, for a regular and much-needed vacation to Barovia. And to Jeremy Forgione, wherever you are, for being the only one to encourage drawing comics on the backs of tests.

Last but certainly not least, I would like to send a UY Scuti-size thank you to the space exploration community of the past, present, and future. Please keep looking to the stars. You're our best bet.